DOCUMENT ON PEACE EDUCATION

DOCUMENT
ON
PEACE EDUCATION

Edited by

Prateeti Barman
Triveni Goswami

AKANSHA PUBLISHING HOUSE
NEW DELHI-110002 (INDIA)

AKANSHA PUBLISHING HOUSE
4649-B/21, Ansari Road
Darya Ganj, New Delhi - 110 002
Ph.: 23263193 / 9811582579 / 09435116718
Fax: 011-23263193
Email: ektabooks@yahoo.com
www.akanshapublishinghouse.com

Document on Peace Education

First Published 2009
ISBN 978-81-8370-158-7

PRINTED IN INDIA

Published by Akansha Publishing House, New Delhi and Printed at Aryan Enterprises, Delhi.

"SINCE WARS BEGIN IN THE MINDS OF MEN AND WOMEN, IT IS IN THE MINDS OF MEN AND WOMEN THAT THE DEFENCES OF PEACE MUST BE CONSTRUCTED."

UNESCO

"TRUE PEACE IS NOT MERELY THE ABSENCE OF TENSION; IT IS THE PRESENCE OF JUSTICE."

MARTIN LUTHER KING JR.

CONTENTS

PART II

ACKNOWLEDGMENTS

This document on peace education is an outcome of a one year action research study titled "Pre-emptive Training in Peace Education: Theoretical and Activism Training " carried out in two hill districts of Assam i.e. Karbi Anglong and N. C. Hills with the sponsorship of North East Network (NEN). We must thank NEN for this sponsorship. We are also indebted to our Director Prof. Indranee Dutta for her support and encouragement. We would also like to thank Prof. A.N.S. Ahmed for his invaluable comments during the study.

We are grateful to a number of people from N.C. Hills and Karbi Anglong who have introduced us to the nook and corner of these districts and made us realize the intensity and magnitude of the situation. We appreciate the help and cooperation of all, including among others, college teachers, civil society members, women from the grass roots, school teachers and school children. We would also like to extend our heartfelt thanks to our coordinators Gulson Teron and Thanuram Teron. It would have been impossible to do our work without their help.

We must also thank all the contributors in this document for their participation in the workshop and specially for their valuable writing on peace education. We would like to thank Ratna Bhuyan and Abhijit Bhuyan for their contribution while preparing the document in the initial phase. A special thanks to Hrishikesh Buragohain for his art work in the document. We would also like to extend our heartfelt gratitude to Arnob Bormudoi for taking time out from his otherwise busy schedule to design the cover for this book.

This document is a collective work of the Peace Studies team. We all enjoyed working together as a team and each visit to these districts helped us in understanding the situation much better. Our effort will be successful only if the state and civil society members realize the need for peace education in this part of the country.

BACKGROUND NOTE

The concept of the culture of peace gained particular relevance during the year 2000, the International Year for the Culture of Peace. This was followed by the decade ahead, 2001-2010, which was proclaimed by the General Assembly as the *International Decade for a Culture of Peace and Non-Violence for the Children of the World.* The International Decade comes amid a number of other such Decades dedicated to bringing attention to important issues, including those directly relevant such as the *Third Decade to Combat Racism and Racial Discrimination (1993-2003), the International Decade of the World's Indigenous People (1994-2004), the United Nations Decade for Human Rights Education (1995-2004) and the United Nations Decade for the Eradication of Poverty (1997-2006).*

In Assam, insurgency in the plains is a recent phenomenon which developed due to popular feelings of neglect and discrimination arising out of ethnic, cultural and historical differences with the people in the hills. After independence, special provisions were made for the indigenous people. It was through the Sixth Schedule of the Constitution of India that an attempt was made for intermixing of the hills and plains people through various socio-cultural activities. The two autonomous district councils i.e. North Cachar Hills and Karbi Anglong were functioning reasonably well. But gradually, across time, they began to demand statehood as provided under Article 244(A) of the Constitution. In the latter half of the 1990s rebel groups like *United Peoples' Democratic Solidarity* (UPDS) and *Dima Halim Daogah* (DHD) came into existence in these hill districts. The unrest and conflict that has followed subsequently has left a deep scar in the minds of the children as well as the adults in these districts of Assam.

This growing backwardness, hatred and alienation among the people of Assam prompted Peace Studies, OKDISCD and North East Network (NEN) to come together and carry out an action research study titled "Pre-emptive Training in Peace Education: Theoretical and Activism Training". This study was carried out in the two hill districts of Assam i.e. Karbi Anglong and North Cachar Hills Districts, which have experienced a severe form of ethnic violence and instability in the recent past. The target groups of this action research were women, children, youth and civil society organizations. The objectives and goals of this action study was—

- To impart pre-emptive training in peace education and peace making;
- To bring people together for conflict transformation and sharpen awareness about peaceful existence between people; and
- Capacity building of the participants.

The aims of Peace Education are manifold and touch upon varying aspects of human relations and personal self-growth. Some of the aims are listed below:

- To understand the nature and origins of violence and its effects on both victim and perpetrator.
- To create frameworks for achieving peaceful, creative societies.

- To sharpen awareness about the existence of hostile relationships between people and within and between nations.
- To investigate the causes of conflicts and violence embedded within perceptions, values and attitudes of individuals as well as within social and political structures of society.
- To encourage the search for alternative or possible non-violent skills.
- To equip children and adults with personal conflict resolution skills.

Peace education has to become an integral part of the formal education system and the National Council of Educational Research and Training (NCERT) and State Council of Educational Research and Training (SCERT) have already begun training teachers to impart value education to the children of India to reduce violence among the children.

This book is the product of the project on "Pre-emptive Training in Peace Education: Theoretical and Activism Training". The purpose of this book is to serve as a resource material for the educators and thereby, disseminate the notion and significance of peace education today. As part of the project, several workshops were organized with the teachers and children especially, on themes related to Peace. A seminar on the theme 'Is Peace Education Necessary in the Current Context?' was organized in February, 2008 wherein several eminent practitioners from the field of education participated and aired their views on the said theme. In this book, an attempt has been made to reflect these expressions into a coherent framework and develop an understanding of the multi-layered notions of peace and conflict. For convenience, this book has been divided into three major parts. The *first* part of the book comprises of the Introduction and a few articles related to the notion of peace and the significance of peace education written by eminent scholars, educators and social activists. The *second* part of the book comprises of a segment on Peace Education and several notions related to peace and conflict. Here, we have tried to include certain selected topics in order to explain what Peace Education is. There is also a segment on Peacemakers from around the world. The two hill districts of Assam have a long history of violence and unfortunately children are also part of it. During the project we tried to read the minds of these young children through their writings, drawings, exchange of dialogues and views on peace. As we consider them to be valuable contributors towards a culture of peace we have tried to include some of their expressions in the *third* part of this book. *Finally*, we have made an attempt to incorporate a few lessons/exercises that we feel might be helpful in imbibing the concept and spirit of Peace in the minds of our children.

While working on this book, an attempt has been made to consult books, journals, reports as well as internet sources to gather information. A special mention may be made of the site *www.wikipedia.com,* an online encyclopaedia, which was consulted for the write-ups on issues related to peace and conflict. We have also made use of diverse sources and materials of the UNO (United Nations Organizations) and various other available guidelines from the country and the world over, so that educators and social activists can make use of them while dealing with the children and adolescents to promote a culture of peace.

PART–I

1

INTRODUCTION

*Anuradha Dutta**

"Averting war is the work of politicians; establishing peace is the work of education".

—*Maria Montessori*

> Peace, in the sense of the absence of war, is of little value to someone who is dying of hunger or cold. It will not remove the pain of torture inflicted on a prisoner of conscience. It does not comfort those who have lost their loved ones in floods caused by senseless deforestation in a neighboring country. Peace can only last where human rights are respected, where the people are fed, and where individuals and nations are free.

These profound words of His Holiness, Dalai Lama placed before mankind is a reality, which indeed must govern the thought of each and every rational being on earth. However, in actuality 'peace' has different meanings within different cultures, as well as different connotations for the sphere in which peaceful processes are generally applied. There is a difference between inner peace and outer peace. Inner peace

*Anuradha Dutta is Professor, Peace Studies, OKDISCD

concerns a state of being and of thinking about others. Outer peace, on the other hand, refers to the natural environment, the culture, international relations, civic communities, families and individuals. So, within each sphere peace has different meanings. In the international sphere - peace refers to peace treaty, a ceasefire or balance of power. For sociologists, peace means cultural norms that legitimize non-violence. In culture, peace is interfaith dialogue and multicultural communication. In a civil society, peace implies a state of full employment, affordable housing, and ready access to health care and educational opportunities. Psychologists deem peace as positive inter personal communication. Whereas for environmentalists, peace is sustainable practice used by a native culture. Thus, peace continues to be the object of unceasing quest in almost all communities and groups.

The real world today, however, depicts another reality about peace, which is rather cruel. It has been found that training of each new generation today centres not on peace, but, more and more on divisive issues of in-group/ out-group differentiations, inter-group conflicts and preparation to fight against real and perceived enemy. As conflict in recent times has overcome peace and has become a part of life, priority has to be given to training and education for conflict management. In recent decades, in different parts of the world, after going through the experience of the devastation of wars, the concept of peace education has indeed gained momentum and is being recognized and accepted as a necessary dimension of a truly democratic society.

Peace Education: In History and Reflection

Peace education like the concept of peace is a contested notion. In order to combat the current culture of discrimination & intolerance in schools the Peace Education programme has been conceived with an aim of cultivating a culture of respect & peaceful co-existence. Betty Reardon, one of the leading peace education experts from the United States who has analyzed more than hundred curricula on peace from Kindergarten through High School, concludes that, "There are as yet no clear and precise limits to, nor standards for what is to be included in peace education". She identifies nine areas to be included in peace education – conflict resolution, cooperation, non-violence, multicultural understanding, human rights, social justice, world resources and global environment. According to Reardon, the purpose of peace education is to promote the development of authentic planetary consciousness that will enable one to function as a global citizen and to transform the present human condition by changing social structure and patterns of thought that have created it. Peace education, therefore is, the transmission of knowledge about requirement of and obstacles to the possibilities of achieving and maintaining peace, training in skills for interpreting the knowledge, and the development of participatory capacities for applying the knowledge.

There have been peace education efforts for over one hundred years now. The understanding of the concept of peace has changed throughout history, and so has its role and importance in the educational system from the very beginning of the institutionalized socialization of children. The end of World War I (1914–1918) brought powerful support for the need of international cooperation and understanding and helped instill a desire to include these ideas in educational systems. The League of Nations and a number of non-governmental organizations worked together on these ideas, especially through the International Institute of Intellectual Cooperation, the Institute that preceded UNESCO.

In history, peace education began after the civil war rising out of concern for destructiveness of modern weapons. Peace education has taken different shapes, as peace educators have attempted to address different forms of violence. After the atomic bomb drops in Nagasaki and Hiroshima, peace educators in Japan in the 1950s led a campaign known as A-bomb education. In the poor countries, peace education is known as Development Education where students learn to address the problems of structured violence. In Ireland, peace education is referred to as 'education for mutual understanding'. In South Korea, peace education is referred to as 'education for reunification'. Later, peace movements began concentrating on stopping the threat of nuclear war, halting the arms race, and encouraging disarmament. The issues of environmental protection and development also found their place in peace education programmes.

The contemporary socio-political environment, the fear of terrorism and the increasing gap between developed and under-developed countries has indeed created new challenges for understanding peace and for the development of the underlying principles of responsibility and security. Thus, it has been found that peace education has developed its own culture according to the situation.

A number of educational initiatives overlap with peace education. These include child rights/human right education, education for development, gender training, global education, life skills education, landmine awareness, and psychosocial rehabilitation. Each can provide a perspective to examine how peace can be mainstreamed in basic education.

In the light of the above observations, Gavriel Salmon rightly summarizes current peace education activities under four categories:

i. Peace education as a matter of changing mindset

ii. Peace education as a matter of cultivating a set of skills

iii. Peace education as a matter of promoting human rights

iv. Peace education as a matter of environmentalism, disarmament, and the promotion of culture of peace

Amidst these different issues and activities which peace education strives to address, Ian Harris identifies ten goals specifically for effective peace education:

i. Appreciate the richness of the concept of peace

ii. Address fear

iii. Provide information about the security system

iv. Understand violent behaviour

v. Develop intercultural understanding

vi. Provide for a future orientation

vii. Teach peace as a process

viii. Promote concept of peace accompanied by social justice

ix. Stimulate respect for life

x. End violence.

All these goals and issucs prove that desire for peace is widespread but there is no agreement in this sphere. It is, therefore, important to develop a theoretical base for peace.

Peace Education: An Approach

Hossain B Danesh identifies four pre requisite conditions for Peace education - changing mindset, cultivating set of skills, promoting human rights and matters related to environmentalism and disarmament, and promoting the culture of peace. For, according to Danesh, peace is a requirement for effective peace education and peace education creates higher states of peace.

There exists a desire for peace but approaches to it, are diverse. In 1996, Robin Burns and Robert Sapsago in their book on Peace Education wrote that the field and theme that are included in peace education are diverse. There is diversity in approaches, underlying philosophies, basic methodology as well as goals. Peace education is full of people with good intentions but without a unique theoretical framework and firm methodology. For peace education, programme specific situations in which programmes held are important. The complex system of society, the circumstance and the context make the field of peace education very active and diverse. Peace education, in fact, rejects the threat and use of force on all levels and is committed to comprehensive means of civil conflict management.

What one needs is a theoretical framework for comprehensive peace education programme. Education has an enormous impact on children, particularly on issues of conflict and peace. Peace education and civilization are two very important components for the stability of any country, which ultimately can lead to human progress. A world where identity, autonomy and displacement are everyday problems, children should be familiarized with these issues. Education hence is the fundamental method of social progress and reform. The primary purpose of peace education should, therefore, be to build people's capacities to recognise, confront, and transform the culture of violence. Central to such a challenge is providing students with the skills, knowledge, and authority they need to inquire and act upon, what it means to live in a substantive democracy...to fight deeply rooted injustices in a society and world founded on systematic economic, racial, and gendered inequalities. Horton and Freire remind one that such social change cannot be forced upon people. Peace education should hence be student-centered, a process of mutual learning among students and educators. Peace education is not only about teaching, it is about helping oneself and others become a peace builder. With peace education, one aims to generate profound compassion for the whole humanity and nurture a form of all encompassing love that enables young people to transcend hatred and build bonds of sisterhood and brotherhood among all people.

Peace education thus encompasses the key concepts of education and peace. Education is defined as a process of systematic institutionalized transmission of knowledge and skills as well as basic values and norms that are accepted in a certain society. Peace education can be defined as an interdisciplinary area of education whose goal is institutionalized. Peace education thus aims to help students to acquire skills of non-violent conflict resolution. Unlike conflict resolution, peace education has a more pro-active approach. Its aim is to prevent conflict in advance or to educate individuals and a society for peaceful existence on the basis of nonviolence, tolerance, equality, respect for difference and social justice.

Peace Education: The Reality

According to the Integrative theory of peace, truly effective peace education can take place in the context of a unity based worldview. Peace education and civilization are inseparable dimensions of human progress. Today, the new generation of youth and children are trained with a conflict-based perspective. Education at home, schools, community and mass media focus on issues of conflict. History textbooks by and large are the accounts of rivalries, wars and conflicts. The issues of co-existence and cooperation, which are fundamental for the formation and maintenance of life, are not taught. Children are given lessons in issues of power, competition, winning and losing. The children are taught that the world is full of competition and only the fittest would survive. As a result, there is today, a new generation matured with ways of conflict, competition and violence. Effective peace education cannot take place with a conflict-based worldview; it has to be based on peace.

There is a need to bring about changes in views. The United Nations Educational, Scientific and Cultural Organization (UNESCO) in 1998 recognized education as the key means to spearhead the movement towards a culture of peace. Till date, not much research has been done on the impact of peace education on society. Though one such study reveals that peace education and peace studies can bring about a difference in value orientation. M Harris in his book on Peace Education mentions that peace education classes have a ripple effect, where one person who acts peacefully influences the behaviour of others and those persons in turn, act in such a way as to inspire others to be more peaceful. However, one must agree that these effects are hard to measure. H B Danesh points out that peace education can best take place in the context of the culture of peace. This culture of peace, according to the U N Charter, is respect for human rights, democracy and tolerance, promotion of development, education for peace, free flow of information and wider participation of women as an integral approach to preventing violence.

Although a significant number of courses covering these subjects were introduced, effectiveness of these programmes was rather low. It seems that the participating students were unwilling to deal with issues like tolerance, democracy and human rights. Looking back at the failures, one gets a sense that this has happened due to the lack of development of the necessary degree of trust and confidence building required at the social level, which is essential in removing stereotypes, misconceptions and flawed information that many teachers, students and parents have about the 'other' group. The discrepancy between theory and practice always has a detrimental impact on students' learning process as it places them in a state of conflict between what is said and what is done. The primary purpose of peace education hence unquestionably is to build peoples' capacities to recognize, confront and transform the culture of violence. They need to fight against the deeply rooted injustice in a society.

Peace education has five postulates

(i) It explains the root of violence

(ii) It teaches alternatives to violence

(iii) It adjusts to cover different forms of violence

(iv) Peace itself is a process that varies according to context

(v) Conflict is omnipresent

Based on these postulates, peace educators, peace academics and peace activists primarily organize their tasks into three interrelated sphere of peace action:

(i) Opposing & confronting violence in all of its manifestation

(ii) Conducting learning & research, acquiring & disseminating new knowledge that is produced towards preparing the citizenry for developing a deeper understanding of violence

(iii) Transforming the cultural, social & political organization that promote and sustain systems of direct & indirect violence

The *social individual* is the final target of the peace education effort. For development of sympathy for others and building trust, developing awareness of interconnectedness with others, is necessary for the development of a positive self. The modern liberal theory puts the individual's equality, values, and rights in the centre of a successfully functioning society. This basic thesis is the beginning of the philosophy and practical protection of human rights. From the individual psychological point of view one thinks in terms of educating a complete person. In the educational system this does not mean transmitting only the facts, but it includes the complete social, emotional, and moral development of an individual; the development of a positive self-concept and positive self-esteem, and the acquisition of knowledge and skills to accept responsibility for one's own benefit as well as for the benefit of society. The development of a positive self-concept is the foundation for the development of sympathy for others and building trust, as well as the foundation for developing awareness of interconnectedness with others. In that sense, a *social individual* is a starting point as well as a final target of peace education efforts.

The Way Out and Forward: Peace Education as Security

The key problem of peace education is not the interpersonal conflict but the collective conflict between groups, races, nations, or states. Therefore, the issue of transferring the positive attitudes towards members of other groups – attitudes achieved in safe environments such as classrooms, schools, workshops, and the like to all members of the out-group and all other out-groups remains the pivotal issue of peace education. Children learn about peace and the need for peace in safe, protected environments and then return to a wider society where there still is injustice, asymmetry of power, a hierarchical structure, discrimination, and xenophobia. Programmes for peace education must not only strengthen the capacity of an individual for critical thinking but also strengthen the individual's ability to resist the majority, if the majority is one that discriminates. As stated by Ervin Staub in 1999, "For change to happen and spread, there is a need for a *minimum mass of people* who share attitudes, a culture in which they can express those attitudes, and a society that accepts the attitudes".

Since the very beginning of the development of systematic peace education, there has been discussion about whether it should be added as a separate programme in schools, or if the principles of peace education should be applied through regular school subjects. The variety of approaches and attitudes on what peace education actually is leads to the introduction of a series of titles, such as multicultural training, education for democracy and human rights, and education for development. Many in the field, however, believe that the implementation of principles of peace education into the institutionalized educational system is a better approach, especially within the subjects encompassing the cultural heritage of the dominant society and the ethnic groups belonging to it. But many also oppose the view.

The educational parties involved in the process of peace education may involve

- Government
- Local businesses
- Board of education officials
- School administration
- School teachers
- Community organization
- Community participants
- Students
- Parents.

These actors will be consulted to assess their interest in the PEP (Peace Education Programme), taking into account the specific need of the community in which the programme will be implemented. This programme is participatory and community engagement is continuous and dynamic.

When Peace Studies, a Chair under Omeo Kumar Das Institute of Social Change and Development, Guwahati initiated an attempt in understanding the essence of peace education, it was found that teachers from various schools in Guwahati city were not willing to incorporate peace education as a separate area of study. According to them, it would be an extra burden for the already over burdened children. They felt that Peace education could be made a part of the already existing programme in schools and colleges only if the existing education programme takes care to incorporate certain values in the syllabi at hand. The Political Science Department of Gauhati University has been rather successful in introducing a two-year course in Peace and Conflict Studies. Of late, National Council of Educational Research and Training (NCERT) and SCERT (State Council of Educational Research and Training) too have developed policies on value education. In areas like North East India where conflicts have become a part and parcel of life, the importance of peace education indeed needs to be re-examined.

Many scholars have provided evidence that education can play a significant role in initiating personal, communal and even structural development that bring qualitative differences in society, economy and polity. Education is a security issue. All education imparted has a social purpose. But one seldom pays attention to the social purpose of learning. Peace education attempts to cultivate learning that transforms the worldview and inspires learners to actively pursue the transformation of the culture of violence. Peace education strives to demonstrate the futility of violence through the cultivation of peace-related values, knowledge, attitude and behaviour. The task of peace education unlike peace research is dissemination of peace knowledge. And this dissemination can take place via five existing postulates in peace education. In the first postulate students learn about the 'other' in order to deconstruct the enemy image. With the kind of ethnic conflict we have, this is of special importance. Postulate two presents different peace strategies that can be used to address the problem of violence. Postulate three explains the dynamic nature of peace education as it shifts its emphasis according to the type of violence. Postulate four embeds peace education theory and practice within a specific culture. Postulate five states that the peace educator cannot eliminate conflict but can provide skill for conflict management. If put in to effect, these postulates through peace education, can contribute perhaps with unprecedented results, towards building a truly peaceful society.

REFERENCES

1. Barash, David P & Webel, Charles P (2007), *"Peace and conflict Studies"* Sage Publications.
2. Reardon, Betty A, *"Tolerance Threshold of Peace,"* UNESCO Publishing, Paris.
3. Solomon, Gavriel & Nero, Baruch (eds.) (2002). *Peace Education: The Concept, Principle and Practice Around the World*, Lawrence Erlbaum Associates, London.
4. Reardon, Betty A (1995). *Educating for Human Dignity: Learning About Rights and Responsibilities*. University of Pennsylvania Press, Philadelphia.
5. Harrie, Ian M & Morrison, Mary Lee (2003). *Peace Education*, McFarland & Co. Inc.

2

INAUGURAL ADDRESS

*Dr. Birendra Nath Datta**

President of the Inaugural Session, Dr. A.N.S. Ahmed, Director of OKD Institute, Dr. Indranee Dutta, Chairperson, Peace Studies of OKD Institute, Dr. Anuradha Dutta, Academic Dignitaries and Learned Participants, Research Scholars, Students and Observers.

When Dr. Anuradha Dutta personally visited me sometime back and requested me to take part in this very important seminar, I readily gave my consent. There were several reasons for doing so. First, I sincerely value the goodwill of Dr. Anuradha Dutta and her commitment to vital social issues. Second, since its very inception the academic programmes of the OKD Institute have aroused in me a very high degree of interest as well as admiration. And third, being myself a believer in the importance of peace with dignity, I thought that by following the proceedings of the seminar I myself would stand to gain as it would give me the opportunity to learn from the wisdom and experience of scholars, educators and activists. But when I came to learn that I was

*Eminent Scholar and Former President of *Asam Sahitya Sabha*

expected to deliver the Inaugural Address, I was really hesitant. Although I felt greatly honoured by the gesture, I had genuine doubts about my own capacity to prove equal to the faith reposed on me. Thus, when I came here this morning and occupied this special seat, I was already considerably shaky. And just now, the high adulations showered on me while introducing me have left me more embarrassed and uncomfortable. I certainly do not deserve all this. I am inclined to think that the decision of the organizers has been prompted more by their respect for my grey hair than by the genuineness of my credentials.

In any case, I feel extremely grateful to all concerned – and particularly to Dr. Anuradha Dutta who has been the running force behind the planning and execution of this programme.

The preliminaries over, I now propose to get down to the business of fulfilling my responsibility of speaking something around the topic of the seminar by way of delivering the Inaugural Address.

The title of the seminar topic has been designed in the form of a query: "Is Peace Education Necessary in the Current Context?" The brief outline on peace education that has been circulated by the organizers makes it eminently clear that the title represents a rhetorical question: it certainly does not call for a negative answer. They are fully convinced that peace education is necessary and that, too, in the world context. But, the present day atmosphere of conflict and violence afflicting North-East India is naturally the immediate concern.

I would like to make my own position on this issue clear by positing two counter-questions;

One : Is peace education not necessary?
Two : Is peace education necessary only in the

current context and more specifically in the context of the turmoil prevalent in the socio-political scenario in North-East India?

What I mean to suggest is that if by peace education we understand the generation and promotion of awareness about the importance of peace in society, such education has its relevance at all times – not only at times of turmoil and disturbance but also during times of comparative calm and tranquillity. Again turmoil and disturbance have various kinds of ramifications at different levels such as local, regional, national and international as has been clearly brought in the outline already circulated and referred to.

Now, by education we normally mean the schooling system. If peace education is thought to be necessary – which we agree it is, - then should it be made a part of the school curriculum? Personally I would not vote for it for more than one reason. For one thing, the school curriculum is already overloaded. There is no point in adding more materials into the bulging school bag under whose weight the backs of our poor little learners are constantly bent. If peace study is included in the syllabus it will just become another dry subject to be learnt in the class room, read in the text book and mechanically memorized for the sole purpose of qualifying for the exams. This would, I believe, serve no meaningful purpose.

Then, again, we have to contend with the atmosphere of the elite school system towards which people of all income groups seem to be rushing headlong. It is a virtual war zone where sympathy, tolerance and cooperation have no room. What matters is competition and rivalry. What guidance does the school-going child get from his mentors? Your class-mate is your adversary. You have to beat him and overtake him. You become an 'achiever' – whatever the cost – and let the society go to hell.

Obviously, such a school system cannot be expected to take us anywhere near our desired goal.

In fact, what is required is not parrot learning of peace lessons but an attitudinal orientation towards the positive role that peace can play in our lives.

If not the school, should the family be the agency for the inculcation of peace education into the child's mental make-up? Formerly, the family did play such a role more or less successfully. Deep and abiding family ties and mutual concern used to be highlighted by the joint family. Neighbourly goodwill and cooperation also set examples for the youngsters. And today? The joint family has practically broken down as far as the educated elite section is concerned. Detachment rather than attachment to anyone outside the nuclear family is the guiding principle to be followed. And as for neighbourly relations, I think the situation is epitomized by the much publicized advertisement of a particular TV brand: "Neighbours envy, owner's pride". If your neighbour has a fashionable TV set, you must have a more spectacular one. If your neighbour has a utility car, you must have a swanky one. Well, one can go on adding more and more examples. So, the family can no longer be expected to be the place where concern for peace can be taught and learnt.

Then, can we turn to religion perhaps? Yes, it is well known that all the major religions have preached and spread the message of peace in their own distinctive ways. Buddhism for example, could certainly be called a pacifist religion – being opposed to all kinds of intolerance, conflict and violence. Similarly, the meaning of the very term Islam, the religion of the Muslims, is peace. The Muslim religion's salutation – assalamu alaiqum – happens to mean "peace be with you"! Jesus Christ, from whom the origin of Christianity is traced, has been the much acclaimed apostle of peace for centuries. And what about Hinduism? Much before the name Hindu came to be attached to it, the sages or *rishis*, who can be called the founding fathers of the religion, uttered impassioned invocations for peace not only in the human society but in the entire universe. Here is an example:

Dyauh śântir antariksam sântih
Prithivi śântir âpah śântir osadhyah śântih
Vansspatayah śântir visve devah śântir brahma śântih
Sarvam śântir śântireva śântih
Sâ mâ śântir edhi

Peace of the sky, peace of the mid-region
Peace of earth, peace of water, peace of plants
Peace of trees, peace of all gods, peace of Brahma
Peace of the universe, peace of peace
May that peace come to me !
(See AC Bose 1970)

But have the religions been able to stop violence and ensure peace? Unfortunately no, in fact, some of the bitterest wars and worst carnages have taken place on the question of religion. Think of the crusades in the Middle Ages. Think of the educated annihilation of Jews in the last century simply because they happened to be followers of Judaism. Think of the bloody encounters that have been going on now between the Israelis and the Palestinians. As we all know, one of the greatest threats to peace the world over in recent times has been what has come to be termed as 'Islamic Terrorism'. Nearer home, we have been frequently witnessing the senseless confrontations being stirred up by Hindu bigotry and Islamic fanaticism.

One of the biggest ironies of history has been connected with the ambivalent relationship between war and peace. The realization that peace deserves a chance has almost always come after some bloody war has been fought with great intensity. The best example is perhaps provided by the Kalinga war and what followed after it was over. After the sacrifice of innumerable lives and the flowing of rivers of blood, it was Ashoka the victor who undertook the biggest peace initiative ever, spreading the message of peace, love and understanding in different parts of the world. In more recent times, big world powers were involved in prolonged international war forces, twice within the span of less than half a century – World War I and World War II – causing untold death, destruction and misery. And each time the realization of the futility of war and the need for peace and cooperation apparently dawned upon the belligerent parties. Such realization led to the establishment of the League of Nations after World War II. And we know how effective these bodies have been! The dark clouds of another holocaust are still hanging over the world's head.

Let us try to take a closer look at the Indian scenario. The conventional history of India as taught in the schools of colleges abounds in accounts of invasions, conquest, power contests and internecine family-feuds. But there have also been major peace processes at different periods of history including the one of Ashoka we have already referred to. There was a big surge in favour of peace in the medieval period when preachers and teachers like Sankardeva, Chaitanyadeva, Kabir, Dadu, Nanak and Namdev had emphasized such values as tolerance understanding and cooperation in different parts of the country. Their teachings are certainly still relevant in the present context and outwardly they are still being venerated by innumerable devotees and followers. But what have we been witnessing as ground realities in the respective areas of their erstwhile operation – in Punjab, in Gujarat, in Maharashtra, for example? And what about our very own Assam? Where the great Sankardeva had brought in a wonderful atmosphere of inclusiveness and synthesis based on humanistic values of compassion and tolerance. One of the most potent causes of conflict and confrontation is the feeling, real or imagined, of being deprived of what is due, of being neglected, of being discriminated against or being somehow marginalized. More often than not such feelings are associated with the question of identity. Amartya Sen has, with his rare insight and persuasive reasoning, shown how false and narrow notions of identity can breed intolerance, hatred, discord and confrontation eventually leading to violence that may take different forms under different circumstances. I am quoting below some relevant passages from his book *Identity and Violence, The Illusion and Destiny* (2006) which, I am sure, will speak for themselves:

> In our normal lives, we see ourselves as members of a variety of groups – we belong to all of them.
>
> (p. XII)
>
> Our shared humanity gets savagely challenged when the manifold division in the world is unified only into one dominant system of classification – in terms of religion, of community, or culture, or nation, or civilization
>
> (p. XIII)
>
> . . . we are *diversely different*. The hope of harmony in the contemporary world lies to a great extent in the clear understanding of the pluralities of human identity, and in the appreciation that they cut across each other and work against a sharp separation along one single hardened line of impenetrable division.
>
> (p. XIV)
>
> With suitable instigation a fostered identity with one group can be made into a powerful weapon to brutalize another.
>
> Indeed many of the conflicts and barbarities in the world are sustained through the illusion of a unique and choiceless identity.
>
> (p. XV)

A sense of identity can be a source of not merely of pride and joy but also of strength and confidence.

And yet, identity can kill – and kill with abandon. A strong – and exclusive – sense of belonging to one group can in many cases carry with it the perception of distance and divergence from other groups. Within-group solidarity can help to feel between group discords. (Pp. 1-2)

The underlying message of the above statements is that the chance of inter-group peaceful existence is maximized when there is the recognition and acceptance of diversity and plurality.

Significantly, there is so much material proclaiming this message in our own Indian heritage of intellectual search which goes back to the Vedas and Upanishads. I had earlier quoted the Vedic *mantra* invoking universal peace. I am reproducing below two other *mantras* which uphold the value of universal friendship as well as of the recognition of diversity and plurality.

Mitrasya mā caksusā sarvāni bhutāni samiksantām
mitrasyāham caksusâ sarvāni bhutani samikse
mitrasya caksusâ samiksamiha

May all beings look on me with the eye of a friend;
May I look on all beings with the eye of a friend.
May we look on one another with the eye of a friend.

(See A.C.Bose, *The Call of the Vedas*,1970, p. 285)

Janain vibhrati bahudha vivacasain
Nanadharmanam prithivi yathaukasain
Sapasrain dhara dravinasya me duhain
Dhruveva dhenur anupasphuranti

May the earth that bears people speaking varied languages,

With various religious rites according to the places of abode,
Enrich me with wealth in a thousand ways
Like a milch cow that never fails.
(See *Ibid*, p. 287)

Have these messages been completely lost for us modern Indians? Not quite. The two leading lights of modern Indian thought – Mahatma Gandhi and Rabindranath – had deeply imbibed the enduring values inherent in the Indian heritage and had interpreted them in their own distinctive way to rediscover their relevance, *not only for us Indians* but also for the world at large. Mahatma Gandhi with his homespun wisdom and moral conviction demonstrated how the moral force of non-violence can be the strongest of weapons to fight against the forces opposed to peace and humanism and can be wielded with great efficacy by the common man with whom he had identified himself. Rabindranath had taken a more sophisticated line of approach but he also like Gandhi transcended the barriers of the local and the national and held high the ideal of world humanity. This vision of Rabindranath is reflected in the motto of the Visva Bharati University which he had established at Santi Niketan – "where the whole world forms its single nest"

(*Yatra visva bharati ekanidam*)

Today both Mahatma Gandhi and Rabindranath happen to be cult figures provoking a lot of high-flown political oratory and hair-splitting intellectual debate. Their portraits and statues are objects of public display. But whether their teaching has any real influence as guiding principles in our public life is anybody's guess. Are they then destined to remain "ineffectual angels"?

I do not want to sound pessimistic: by no means. I have always kept my faith in man's capacity to be humane. But at the same time, I believe in taking a pragmatic position and not being carried away by emotionally charged idealistic fervour. As things stand today, the prospects of peace appear to be none too bright. But yet I am convinced that hope must be kept alive and the search for peace must continue whatever the challenges.

3

IS PEACE EDUCATION NECESSARY IN THE CURRENT CONTEXT?

A Brief Paper with Special Reference to North Cachar Hills, Assam

*Vanlal T. Bapui**

In order to establish the need for peace education, we need to re-examine as to what we mean by peace and then go on to state the problems in the context. In this brief paper I will try to present some of my thoughts and views.

What do we mean by peace? The Dictionary gives the meaning of peace as "a state of quiet, freedom from disturbance, freedom from war, cessation of war, a treaty that ends war, freedom from contention, ease of mind or conscience, tranquility, quiet, stillness, silence" in the noun

*The writer is a retired Headmaster, a Social Worker and Litterateur and lives in Haflong, N.C. Hills, Assam

form. The meaning is quite comprehensive and each of the individual meanings given deserves detailed discussion and explanation. However inclusive and comprehensive these may be, yet there still seems to be something wanting.

We all know that peace does not mean an absence of wars or conflicts alone. It has something to do with the mind and attitudes of people. In the deepest sense, peace is a sense of goodwill towards others, wishing them the best in life. There is love and concern for others, not only as human beings, but as brothers and sisters whose happiness and welfare directly affects a person. It is also the promotion of a sense of belonging in that, the suffering and sorrows of others are shared with concern and steps are taken for the redress of those sufferings. In short, peace wants the complete well-being of a person in relation to others.

In today's society, such considerations are hardly seen in the lives of people. Our life and lifestyles appear to be heading towards concern for the individual only. There is no consideration for the other person as a human being. The attitude that we can see is that if it is ok for me, it is right and good. I have nothing to do with the lives of others. Even in business and trading practices, many people are involved in selling drugs, guns, explosives and other destructive substances knowing that these are things that will bring ruin to the life of other people. Not to speak of concern, our respect for and consideration of other's lives have become so little, that human lives are reduced to having no value or meaning. There is no concern whatsoever for human life as human beings.

North Cachar Hills District has been the peaceful abode of a number of different communities belonging to the hill tribes. The first three quarters of the last century saw the peaceful and steady development of the land and its people. But the last quarter of the century saw something else in the form of violence, unhealthy competitions, unwanted elements in the society, the unthinkable was happening at a pace so fast that before anyone could do anything, it had swept everyone in its grip. And now the peaceful situation of the District has been reduced to being one of the most volatile and violent areas of our state. One can hear the news of killings almost every week and sometimes even in daily incidents. The dawn of the 21st century for the District appears to be spelling certain doom. In spite of the fact that we have successfully elected our representatives to the Autonomous Council and have returned a new government, the situation is becoming worse everyday. At the moment, people are at the mercy of others who are making a living out of their hard earned incomes. I know of many innocent persons who are compelled to part with their life savings and the fruits of their toils. Even at this time people say that the *annual tax collections* are going on. Even small business entrepreneurs like roadside *paan* shops and tea stalls are not spared. In this kind of situation, humanly speaking, to have concern and goodwill for others, is unthinkable. The next person on the street may be the one who is trying to get something from you through extortion. One never knows. In recent times, there has been a spate of kidnapping for ransom leading to the killing of the abducted persons. It is said that even after some portion of the ransom demanded is paid off, they are still killed. One may never know the truth, but people on the street seem to be fully aware of such things.

Under such circumstances, the need for peace education is all the more necessary and urgent. But peace is not a subject which should be learnt and memorized for use at certain times only. It is to be practiced in life at all times. Small gestures, discussions, deeds etc. help to cultivate peace. Hence in peace education, the inculcation of simple deeds and positive attitudes towards life need to be formed in order to promote peace. To speak words of encouragement and to praise rather than criticize, to help others resolve differences, to apologize for mistakes or hurt caused to others, to express feelings honestly and peacefully with respect to others, to listen without defending and speak without judgment, commit not to use violent language or means to settle things etc. may seem commonly understood things, but in reality these are not easy to practice.

In promoting peace, different religious communities may play important and positive roles. In North Cachar Hills, during and after, the ethnic conflict between Dimasas and Hmars, the Presbyterian Church of India initiated a number of peace meetings and had helped in bringing about reconciliations between the warring tribes. Even now, a meeting is being planned in April, 2008 in Haflong wherein tribe leaders, religious communities, NGOs and Govt. officials will be invited to learn together the idea and practice of peaceful co-existence. The theme for the day's workshop will be "Growing together in a multi-cultural society like North Cachar Hills" and they will be encouraged to stand up in unity against violence and subversive activities. Moreover, in all religions, there are peace prayers which the adherents of the religion can pray honestly. I like an ancient Hindu prayer, in which prayers for peace for creation, herbs and forest have been included. A rough translation in English runs as follows –

Om Shanti, Shanti, Shanti,
May all the things in the world be happy
May all the beings in the world be happy
May herbs be wholesome
And may trees and plants bring to all Shanti
May all beneficent beings bring to us Shanti
May the law propagate peace through the entire world
May all things be a source of peace to us
And may thy peace itself, bestow peace on all
And may that peace come to me also.
Om Shanti, Shanti, Shanti.

4

METHODS OF PEACE EDUCATION

*Tom Mangattuthazhe**

Despite the tremendous advances in science and technology in the twentieth century, the dawn of the new millennium has witnessed violence, terrorism, wars and conflict all over the world. The negative trends in social environment have been manifested in the crime level, violence, drug abuse, and the behavioural problems of children in schools and colleges.

As citizens and educators concerned with the possibilities of enacting change toward nurturing a culture of peace we face an essential problem: discussions regarding the responses and policies related to violence, security and peace take place at the highest levels far away from the grassroots, whose participation is necessary and crucial for ensuring equitable outcomes to local and global decision-making.

Education must instill the fundamental human values. The higher life which makes man human and a fit candidate for the enfoldment of the Divinity that is His reality, depends on the cultivation of the cardinal virtues – Truth, Right

*Tom Mangattuthazhe, Secretary, DCPF, tmangatt@gmail.com

Conduct, Love, Peace and Non-violence. These virtues elevate the individual as well as the society of which he is a part.

Methods of Peace Education

The following components can be used for peace education: Theme for the week (Quotations/Positive thoughts/Prayer), Silent sitting, Story-telling, Song and Group activities.

Theme for the Week

This is the focus of the whole lesson and may be represented by a quotation, prayer or poem. This component is a powerful tool that can be used in the assembly and can help to counterbalance the negative images transmitted to children through TV, etc. Children are asked to discuss the theme or quotation as appropriate.

Silent Sitting

Children are encouraged to sit quietly for a few minutes every day. It is a very powerful tool because with constant practice, children become more receptive and intuitive. It is recommended that every class should start, if possible, with a couple of minutes of this exercise.

Story Telling

Story telling is an ancient art. Long before the introduction of writing, information was passed down in the form of stories. Most religious and world leaders have used story telling to explain and illustrate their teachings. Stories have a deep effect on children. Something told in the form of stories will be remembered and treasured, which otherwise might soon have been forgotten.

Group Singing

The importance of music is increasingly recognized. In the education of the future, music for every person will be deemed as necessary as reading and writing is at present, for it will be clearly seen that it is a most powerful means for bringing life, health and strength.

Most children like to sing, but may be shy to sing on their own. Singing creates a joyful atmosphere and is a good way of creating unity, harmony and self-confidence in children. The effect of a song remains with the person long after the class is over and the values that are in the lyrics will remain in the child's consciousness for a long time.

Group Activities

Group activities consist of two words: Group and Activities. These words convey their meaning and importance.

Integration of values in the Curriculum subjects and Extra-curricular Activities

The subjects are taught according to curriculum requirements. However it is still possible to integrate the teaching of values in all the subject areas.

Play for Peace is a global organization, which brings together children, youth and organizations from various communities. They teach people to be leaders for peace and how to live and play together in creating more peaceful communities.

Play is one of the primary ways that human beings learn as part of the community development initiatives. Play for Peace seeks to prevent violence in conflict-torn areas by teaching people to live together, play together, and work together, they use play to promote relationships among people whose communities suffer from a history of cross-cultural tensions. It was recognized as a "Gift to Humanity" at the Parliament of World Religions in Cape Town in December, 1999.

5

A GLANCE AT PEACE EDUCATION AND ITS MODELLING IN NORTH EAST INDIA

*Atanu Dey**

Peace Education and its Essentiality

Is peace education necessary? Obviously it can have only one small but very affirmative answer, 'yes', because at a time when the entire world is engulfed with *peacelessness* and violence and there are relentless efforts in all spheres to halt this grip of *peacelessness* and restore the order of peace, peace education is yet another means to the path to peace. The efficacy of peace education is to create the environment of peace by nurturing the young minds and adults to avoid conflicts and violence and to live in harmony and tolerance so as to meet the very essence of peace education as defined in the Working Paper of UNICEF 'Peace Education in UNICEF' published in June 1999. This paper defines peace education as the process of promoting the knowledge, skills, attitudes and values needed to bring about behaviour changes that will enable children, youth and adults to

*The writer is a social activists from Karbi Anglong, Assam

prevent conflict and violence, both overt and structural; to resolve conflict peacefully; and to create the conditions conducive to peace, whether at an intrapersonal, interpersonal, inter group, national or international level.[1]

In the beginning of their book 'Peace Education (Second edition)' authors Ian M. Harris and Mary Lee Morrison have highlighted different approaches to peace and have shown how peace education can be the viable alternative to all other approaches. The approaches are:

1. Peace through strength
2. Peace through justice
3. Peace through transformation (pacifism)
4. Peace through politics (institution building).
5. Peace through sustainability and
6. Peace education.

While all the first five strategies have different short comings and difficulties associated with them, peace education does not have any such, though long term solution with this strategy is difficult to evaluate.[2]

So, peace education proves itself as the most effective and flawless approach for establishment of peace.

History of Peace Education in the West

If we look at the history of peace education, we may not find anything in particular incorporated as 'peace education' as part of the school curricula but peace related disciplines such as moral education, environment education, scriptures, value education etc. have always been a part of the curricula. World religions and their prophets were the early peace educators on the face of the civilization. Moses, Lao Tse, Jesus Christ, Gautam Buddha, Baha'ulla all carried the messages of peace with them. The meaning of the word Islam is rooted in *Salema*, meaning peace, purity submission and obedience. The Hindus still follow the practice of praying for peace to be bestowed upon every thing in the universe, while performing any ritual. Down the ages, Comenius, the Czech educator of the 17th century first saw that the road to peace was through universally shared knowledge. In his book, 'Perpetual Peace', Immanual Kant established that, peace could be achieved by constructing legal and judicial systems. In the beginning of 20th century, peace societies were formed in US and Europe to lobby their governments against sabre rattling which led to the World War I. In the inter bellum, peace education fast became a part of general education. Educators and social science teachers used international studies to help draw the citizens of the world together. At this time, Maria Montessori's name occupies a prominent place in correlating peace and education together. She saw that, peace depended on an education that would free the children's spirit, promote love of others and remove the climate of compulsory restriction. In the post World War II period, the first academic peace studies program was established in 1948 at Manchester College, Indiana. The Vietnam war and then the nuclear race and cold war era stimulated more and more University and college programmes which had a unique, international focus directed to warn of the impending devastation.[3]

So, though the modern concept of peace education was more or less shaped in the west in the post world-war era and bore the brunt of the two wars, it not only aimed at eliminating the possibility of global extinction (through world wars and nuclear war at the beginning and at the present time), it also addressed the broader objective of building and sustaining a culture of peace. In the post-world-war period, there had been some other factors which were prevalent in solidifying the concepts of peace education. In a very fast developing world, the emphasis was on imparting more textual knowledge and more skill. Stress was on the cognitive learning than on the development of the child's emotional, social or humanistic aspects. This resulted in the complication of the young mind in many ways and the element of stress was also one of the severe outcomes. In the post 9/11 era, the very basic concept of peace has changed and peace education has become indispensable and essential to drive out the widespread insecurity that has filled the human mind throughout the world.

Peace Education in India

The modern conceptualization and shaping of peace education developed in the west. In India we did not find much about peace education or its efficacy in the entire span of 20th century. Of course, our great educators continued to emphasizes education for peace and peace education. Mahatma Gandhi always observed that *'If we have to preach real peace in this world and carry on real war against war; we shall have to begin with children.'* At one time, moral studies used to be a part of the curricula, but in the fast developing era, it gave way to an increasing emphasis on knowledge-based subjects which seemed to be so essential in coping with the world. The trend continued, and there was more unrest, agitation and violence in all aspects. The separatist movements in North East, Kashmir and Punjab began brewing. Naxalite movements also sprouted elsewhere in the country like the undercurrent. There have been sporadic demands for smaller states in many places which took the form of agitations. Islamic militancy began to make its presence felt in many places. Perhaps all other approaches to peace had been tried, but not peace education.

The UNESCO Prize for Peace Education has been awarded annually since 1981. Mother Teresa had been a recipient of this prize way back in 1992 but that hardly created any ripple in the formation of public awareness about the notion of peace education.

It is only after the 9/11 that we, with the rest of the world started looking anew at the horrors of violence and terror. The Godhra massacre and post-Godhra violence to a great extent created an urge for the search of peace from within. Gradually we started realizing the need for peace education in our schools and colleges.

UNICEF published a working paper on 'Peace Education in UNICEF' in June 1999 which served as a very basis for peace education at the primary level for many countries including India. UNESCO held a seminar in Colombo in January 2001 on peace education to mobilize the awareness in peace education in SAARC countries followed by launching of a teachers' guide to peace education titled "Learning the Way of Peace" in association with the parliamentarians' forum in March 2002.[4] Nirmala Niketan College of Social Work, New Marine Lines in Mumbai was the leading educational institute to impart peace education in Mumbai in December 2002.[5] The same year, City Montessori School in Lucknow was selected for the UNESCO prize for Peace Education. The school strives to inculcate in students the philosophy of 'Jai Jagat' (Glory be to the World!). In February 2005, NCERT did a thorough review of the National Curriculum Framework (NCF), when some basic changes were made to the curricula and introduction of peace education was seriously considered for the first time and the need for the teachers to be given certain broad parameters and emphasis on conflict-resolution.[6] In April 2006, NCERT decided to train teachers in conflict resolution techniques and ways to undermine violence and aggression. For the first time, NCERT organized an orientation programme for teachers that included techniques of conflict management and controlling arrogance and during aggression.[7] Since then, NCERT is organizing such trainings during June-July every year and this, to a large extent, is the beginning of formal peace education in India.

Modelling of Peace Education in the North East

After making a journey through the evolution of peace education in the west and then, after the awareness in India, a question arises, whether there should be any structural or functional difference in peace education in the context of west, India or north eastern part of India? Is not peace education a versatile subject?

While the very philosophy and spirit of peace education remains intact, its practical rendering must be adopted in the local context. The website of IIT Guwahati which organized a National Seminar on Peace in Dialogue, Reflections on North-East India on 1st and 2nd February, 2007 says, "*An important point in understanding Peace is to override the assumption that because conflicts share some general patterns, they ought to be universal and applicable across culture and context. The arrogance of this approach notwithstanding, we have ample evidence now that universal models not only fail but also tend to trigger resentment among communities, especially at the grassroots level. As a result, in recent years, several scholars have begun to address questions of identity and difference in conflict, conflict resolution and peace-building*".[8] So is with peace education. The scope and prospect of peace education in this part of the country must address specifically to the causes and issues which mar peace here.

The issues which perturb peace and cause unrest, agitation and violence in this part of the country are:

- An apprehension that the centralist rulers are out to assimilate the indigenous culture into the mainland culture.
- Domination of the armed forces in the name of restoration of peace.

- Fear of jeopardizing the local identity by the migration of people from other part of the country in large size.
- Unabated influx from neighbouring countries.
- Inter-ethnic conflict among the inhabitants regarding establishment of rights, mainly territorial.
- Inadequate return (royalty) for harnessing of local resources.
- Apartheid mentality of the central rulers towards development of the region in comparison to other part of the country.

There may be some more reasons along with these, which are also responsible.

So, there are grievances, anguish, resentment and aspirations. All these together cause agitation in the public mind and some times find expression in the form of demonstration and terror activities. The genuine aspirations of people get confused and lose direction.

So, the peace education in this part of the country can do a great lot in streamlining and regulating the people's aspirations. It should address the regional issues properly and discuss them thoroughly so as to provide sufficient and adequate information.

Often, there are myths overriding the factual information and there is one-sided information on many issues. Peace education should take care to reveal the truth behind the myths and provide balanced information to all unaddressed issues.

In the information age, peace education should deal with facts, figure and statistics. Peace education must nurture a sense to maintain the scope for unhindered development besides expression of grievance.

Not all the rays of hope are bleak yet. We still sway with the beat of *cheng* of the Karbis, *madols* of the Adivashis or *pepas* of the Assamese or even at the blare of the indi-pop and modern songs. It is amazing to note that, we still love to live with music and songs. Peace education should look at how music can help repose the ambience of peace here.

In the present juncture of time, when the developing economies are striving to attain and maintain a near double digit growth rate, peace education in the part of the world must make us feel that, we have almost missed the bus and any further delay would simply put us behind forever.

Problem of unemployment is always thought to be a major reason for unrest in north east India. The functional aspect of peace education should also focus on new ideas of employment generation in the fast changing era.

In the 21st century, the concept of peace and life should not be confined to the domain of human species only. It must spread beyond human beings to encompass all living beings.

Perhaps, all the issues highlighted above are not covered in the core matter of peace education, but since peace education is a holistic approach towards peace and any approach to peace can only materialize with the local issues in the back ground, these issues should be considered while modelling a peace education policy here. May be, it appears like some one's long wish list, but how else can one express his long unfulfilled desire for peace when all other approaches to peace fail and peace education brings the only ray of hope.

REFERENCES

1. Fountain, Susan (1999), *Peace Education in UNICEF,* Working Paper, Education Section, Programme Division, UNICEF, New York.
2. Harris, Ian M & Morrison, Mary Lee, *Peace Education (Second Edition),* McFairland & Co., pp. 15-19.

3. Soloman, Gavriel & Nero, Baruch (eds), (2002), *Peace Education—The Concept, Principles & Practices Around the World*, Lawrence Erlbaum Associates, London.

4. UNESCO Guide Defines Peace Education, *The Times of India*, March 11, 2002 (TNN).

5. "College Offers Course in Peace Education", *The Times of India*, January 6, 2002 (TNN).

6. *NCERT Plans of Sensitize Children on Gender, Peace*, The Times of India, February 18, 2005 (TNN).

7. '*Peace Education*' to be Introduced in Schools, *The Indian Express*, April 25, 2006 (PTI).

8. National Seminar on *Peace in Dialogue*, Reflections on North-East India, Indian Institute of Technology, Guwahati in collaboration with Indian Council of Social Science Research. February 1 & 2, 2007.

   http://www.iitg.ac.in/conferences/hss_conf.htm

6

NECESSITY OF PEACE EDUCATION

*Sr. Deepthy Rose**

Introduction

Our contemporary times are full of discussions on peace. Discussions revolving around issues of human brotherhood, equality, welfare of all and absence of wars and conflicts are all a part of the larger concern for stable, abiding peace. Why should there be peace? If struggle for survival is the universal law of nature and conflict is necessarily written into this struggle which binds human as well as non-human life, why should man aspire for peace contrary to his nature? More importantly why should one man love another in an age of technology and life based on competitive spirit and material progress? In the Northeast too, we have talked about peace for a very long time.

There is no denying the fact that man like any kind of living being is biologically born and is governed by the inexorable necessity of struggling for survival. In the course

*A.C. Headmistress, Don Bosco H.S. School, Diphu

of the struggle for survival, in man, just as in the case of other living beings, man's self interest is apt to be in conflict with what one man calls, his other regarding drives. In most cases of such conflict, self-interest is seen to triumph over the interest of others.

Peace is something that every one seems to want, but that which is difficult to achieve. Various attempts have been made at various levels through out the globe to make it peaceful. But it seems as if the more ardently we try, the more it slips away. People therefore, 'pray for peace' today which, we could say is the only solution, where God can resolve peace on earth as many religious believe. But I am not entering into this kind of solution for I still consider the fact that peace is something that can be achieved provided people really want it.

The need for Peace Education

In today's society, children are exposed to a vast amount of violence, both in the media and in their own lives. It has been said that on television alone, children will see over 8,000 murders and 10,000 other acts of violence by the time they finish school. So if we do not stand up for our children and teach them the skills to live peacefully, who will? If we do not teach our children peace, someone else will teach them violence.

The noble tasks of teachers are–

- To create peaceful environments in our homes and schools where children can feel safe and loved.
- To build the community both in our neighbourhoods and classrooms.
- To encourage children to stand up for their rights and the rights of others.

- To teach children responsibility for their actions and their world.

Peace education is the means to change the future from a culture of violence to a culture of non-violence. One way to ensure that, is to include peace education in our formal and non-formal educational programs in the form of human rights, democracy, non-violence, conflict resolution and justice.

The definition of peace should include cooperation, justice and reconciliation; peace between individuals, groups, peace which is achieved by non-violent means and not by gun.

Peace and conflict resolution are very important subjects for our children to learn and schools have a key responsibility in leading them towards new hope. Children reflect what they read in schoolbooks and mirror their teachers by observing their behaviour and their ways of dealing with conflict. If teachers use physical punishment or prevent students from expressing themselves or giving their opinions, children will do the same with their friends or younger fellows. So the first target should be the classroom curriculum and teachers. Before we educate children we should educate ourselves, not only on how to deal with conflict after it happens, but also on how to avoid it at different levels: interpersonal, intra-personal, inter-community, intra-community, and regional. Most of these conflicts contain personal and cultural aspects that could be avoided if the educational system prepares students by teaching ethics, values, communication skills and how to respect other cultures and races.

Is it really necessary to teach peace? The entire education is geared towards peace. Isn't it already in the curriculum? Are we giving adequate attention today to teach peace? Are our schools really interested in producing a peaceful young generation?

Violence is emerging in an unprecedented manner in our country. Looking at different parts of our country any sensible person feels disheartened and even horrified to see the kind of violent acts being committed by human beings against humanity and nature. It is sad to realize that we live in an era of unprecedented violence in the forms of terrorism, war, crimes, injustice and oppression and exploitation amidst a seemingly outward development enjoyed by a few. The majority of our population lives in stark poverty, struggling for mere survival.

The saddest part of the story is that this state of disorder and confusion in the society is affecting our children. Children naturally absorb the spirit of violence in the atmosphere and will soon grow to be the next generation of perpetrators of violence. Therefore the need to nurture peace in the hearts of children is an imperative today.

Historical Note on Peace Education

Every culture regards peace as a noble ideal to live and attain. However at the beginning of the 20th century, through the guise of a scientific outlook to education, moral and human values including peace were slowly discouraged from school curricula and the entire educational system was viewed narrowly as teaching facts of various subjects and merely providing information with regards to various subjects.

However, despite the materialistic opinions that governed the school curriculum, there were individuals like Maria Montessori and Tolstoy who recognized and valued peace education. Today we are rediscovering her vision of peace education which she tried to reinforce during her era. She opined that peace is the guiding principle of man and nature. And any attempts to divert from this principle will only lead to acts of violence and destruction.

If we study the societies, which lived in relatively peaceful periods of history, we find that the fundamental basis for the peace was a general will for peace, created in its turn by the resolute concern of the custodians of their tradition – in many cases, the elders of the communities. For instance there was a value consensus in matters of intra and inter community relations. Common notions of justice and ideal human conduct enable people with linguistic, ethnic and religious differences to live in peace and goodwill with their political systems. Whether there was ever a period of complete peace or not, what should bother us now is the lack of it in the present times. So our search for peace is really rooted in a search for peace of our times. But I am still convinced that what I refer to as the "original" meaning of peace is worth exploring, and that the human condition is reduced to something quite different, if peace in this sense is no longer a basic aspiration for humans.

Why Peace Education?

If violence begins in the minds of people, so should the foundation of peace be laid in the hearts of human beings. We need to begin building counter forces against violence in our minds. This is to ensure that our attitudes are structured towards re-affirming the images of peace. This is a great responsibility for our educational system and poses a challenge for future curriculum development. Education plays an important role in the process of peace building because it reflects and transmits our societal values and norms from one generation to another.

The Aims of Peace Education

Children do not, of course, come to school unaware of the world in which they live. Schools merely intervene in an ongoing educational process—that of childhood socialization, by which children learn what is expected of their culture and gender. It is also important to challenge openly some of the negative values that underpin our society, such as the explicit acceptance of violence, institutionalized fanaticism, ethnic conflicts, media violence, and the stress on ever-continuing consumerism. Peace education can be based on a variety of assumptions:

1. Violence and violent conflicts are not conducive to human well-being.
2. Violence and conflicts are not inevitable aspects of human nature.
3. Peace is an alternative way of being, behaving, and organizing life in the world.

Therefore, the aims of peace education is to develop the knowledge, attitudes, and skills which are needed in order to explore concepts of peace both as a state of being and as an active process; to enquire into the obstacles of peace and the causes of *peacelessness*, both in individuals, institutions, and societies; to resolve conflicts in ways that will lead towards a less violent and a more just world; to explore a range of different alternatives in particular ways of building a more just and sustainable world society.

Education about Peace and Education for Peace

Education about peace deals with creating awareness about peace and the complexities of peace making. It is to empower people with information necessary for effecting change and building peace in the society. This can be achieved through formal and informal education, including the media. The media plays a significant role in sensitizing people on peace building.

Education for peace deals with teaching skills and creating new structures and attitudes that would facilitate peace making. Since the purpose of peace education is to mobilize the society to bring about conditions necessary for sustainable peace, our educational focus should be reviewed by modifying existing structures such as the curriculum towards peace building.

Tips for Teachers

1. Model tolerance and compassion. Children take their emotional cues from the significant adults in their lives. Avoid making negative statements about any racial, ethnic, or religious group at these very tense and troubling times in our children's lives. Reach out to your neighbours and colleagues who might feel at risk right now because of their ethnicity.

2. Provide useful information. Accurate information about the people, events, reactions, and feelings is empowering. Use language that is developmentally appropriate for children. Make sure that all information is factually true.

3. Avoid stereotyping people or tribes.

4. Address the issue of blame factually. Use non-speculative terms.

5. Discuss how it would feel to be blamed unfairly by association. Ask children if they have ever got in trouble for something a sibling or friend did and how they felt. Would they like it if their entire class were punished for the actions of one student and if they think this would be fair?

6. Explore children's fear. Even children who can describe what happened may not be able to express fears, questions, or describe assumptions or conclusions they may have made. Use activities, role-playing, and discussions to explore their fears about the events and their feelings about various ethnic groups.

7. Emphasize positive, familiar images of diverse ethnic groups. Identify people of diverse ethnicities that your children know and who have a positive place in their

lives. These could be neighbours, friends, school personnel, health care professionals, members of their faith community, or local merchants. Discuss the many characteristics, values, and experiences the children have in common with these people.

8. Undertake projects to help those in need with people from diverse backgrounds. Helping others is part of the healing process. Working with classmates or members of the community who come from different backgrounds not only enable children to feel that they are making a positive contribution, it also reinforces their sense of commonality with diverse people.
9. Learn about the diverse communities and faiths represented in your area. Knowledge debunks myths about other people and can humanize other cultures. In school, have children share information about their family or cultural customs to reinforce the notion that all people have special beliefs and rituals.
10. Read books with your children that address prejudice, tolerance, and hate. There are many, many stories appropriate for varying age groups that can help children think about and define their feelings regarding these issues. The school or local librarian can make recommendations.

Inspirational Quotes on Peace

There is no trust more sacred than the one the world holds with children. There is no duty more important than ensuring that their rights are respected, that their welfare is protected, that their lives are free from fear and want and that they grow up in peace. ***Kofi A. Annan, Secretary – General of the United Nations.***

Peace is not the product of a victory or a command. It has no finishing line, no final deadline, and no fixed definition of achievement. Peace is a never-ending process, the work of many decisions. **Oscar Arias.**

We have grasped the mystery of the atom and rejected the Sermon on the Mount. Ours is a world of nuclear giants and ethical infants. We know more about war than we know about peace, more about killing that we know about living. **General Omar Bradley.**

Peace we want because there is another war to fight against poverty, disease and ignorance. **Indira Gandhi.**

7

NEED FOR PEACE EDUCATION

*Maya Choudhury**

Mahatma Gandhi's name is synonymous with Peace. Yet so strange are the ways of the world that though he lived and died for peace he became the target of violence. When announcing the news of Gandhi's death Jawaharlal Nehru said, "The light has gone I said, but I was wrong, for the light that shone was no ordinary light. The light will illumine this country and the world for many years to come, for the light represents the living truth".

On the 15th of June 2007 the United Nations adopted a resolution moved by India and supported by 142 members, to declare October 2nd the birth anniversary of the Mahatma as the International Day of Non-Violence. This single act of the comity of Nations coming together in support of the Gandhian principle of Non-Violence bears testimony to the vigour and insight that informs the quest for a new vision being shaped by Bapu. It has the potential for transformation, leading to a global non-violent awakening.

Sixty years has passed since India became independent.

*Principal, Maria's Public School, Guwahati, Assam

A whole new generation has blossomed and is forging ahead. With a population of 1.2 billion India is the world's largest Democracy. It is an open and vibrant society and many say that India holds the key to the new world. While it aspires to transform a developing country into a developed nation and become a global leader by 2020, it is beset with some very critical problems – extreme social inequality, employment insecurities, growing energy and water crisis, degraded environment, global warming, a galloping HIV/AIDS epidemic and terrorist attacks that defy the imagination.

Major issues have to be addressed –as the battles for the future of India multiply, as different stakeholders demand different ways of doing things, the way forward is becoming increasingly unclear and thorny. For every swanky shopping Mall that springs up in a booming city, a neglected village explodes in Naxalite rage, for every affluent child who takes wings to study in a foreign university, there are tens dropping out from school, for every fancy eatery a debt ridden farmer is hanging himself and his hope by a rope.

Your and my generation have not handled these differences well. While jostling for our place among the successful we have sought to settle scores with violence, we have been intolerant of differences, insensitive to the needs of others and dismissive of the opinion of those who are not of our own. The time to change has come. We have a chance now to demonstrate to the world that it is possible to lift hundreds of millions of people out of poverty and prove that multiethnic, multi-religious democracy is not a luxury for only rich societies. India could be that liberal democracy that has allowed every citizen including her poor and backward, the freedom to realize their full potential.

The hope perhaps lies with our children, the building blocks of any nation. There is a need to sensitize these young and impressionable minds with 'Peace Education'. India's biggest asset is her young population and if the youth could be empowered to play a constructive role to fight injustices and remove inequalities and in Gandhi's words. . . "To work for an India in which the poorest shall feel it is their country, in whose working they have an effective voice, an India in which there is no high or low class people, an India in which all communities will live in harmony and women will enjoy the same rights as the men", who can stop India from becoming a world leader? However to translate this dream of the Mahatma, to give India a human face, is our greatest challenge.

A few yeas ago a unique movement called education for peace began among the warring communities of Bosnia-Herzegovina. Ever since, several governments, organizations and even the UN have acknowledged the transformative impact of the programme. Education for peace challenges us to question our most profound conception of ourselves, our relationships with others and develop new ways to envision our world and help build peace communities.

If we the educators can consciously facilitate our students to discover their own identity and try to understand the world around them, it will help the children to formulate their own views of the world and help them to articulate their own emotions. Dispute and conflict are inevitable but violence is not. To prevent continued cycles of violence, education must seek to promote peace and tolerance and not fuel hatred and suspicion.

In School, opportunities to introduce all the components of education for peace exist in all subjects. For example when lessons on war are taught in History it is important not to give the students a biased version but to allow free discussions and airing of opinions with a gentle reminder of the causalities caused by war – while teaching Geography, issues ranging from urban development to conflicts over oil, water and land can be touched upon. In science classes both the positive and negative uses of science can by discussed.

Child-centered and participatory methods of learning such as 'Circle Time' are well suited to learning methods for peace education.

Through project work done either alone or in groups, children can explore issues and problems that are important to them. This helps them to make sense of and develop thinking and responding to issues around them. Education for peace enhances young people, spiritually, morally, socially and culturally.

Initially peace was defined as absence of violence; the emphasis was on direct violence – cases of assault, torture, terrorism or war. Today the attention has shifted to causes leading to violence – racism, sexism, hunger, derailment of human rights etc. Today we aim at co-operation and non-violent changes with a focus to create a more equitable and just society.

The aims of Peace Education are briefly to –

- Explore concepts of peace
- Enquire into obstacles of peace and the causes of peacelessness
- Resolve conflicts in a way that will lead to a better world
- Find ways to build a better society and help children to develop a lively and enquiring mind, be able to question and argue rationally.
- Instil respect for all religions and value tolerance for other's ways of life
- Help students to understand the world we live in and the interdependence of individual groups and nations.

To achieve the above we must arm our youth with enhanced skills, inculcate correct values and attitudes and help better understanding and knowledge –

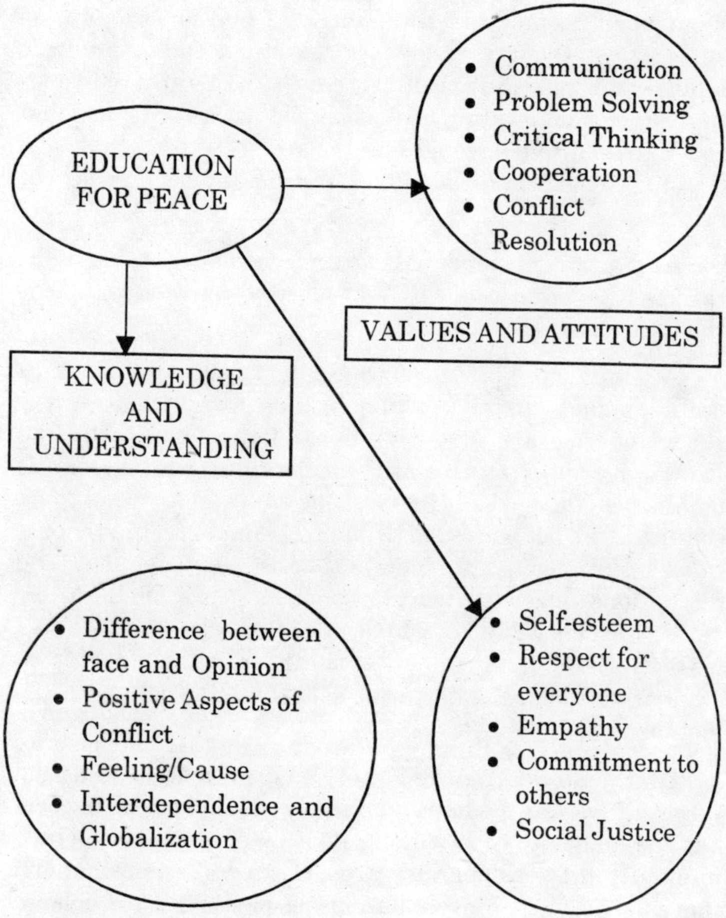

The decades long separatist movement has left the North-East badly scarred. With kidnapping, extortion, violence and unemployment are also on the rise. The ground realities today are so grim that there is weak faith in the notion that good grades and school degrees will put bread on the table. Easy money can be made at the point of a gun and corruption stares you in the face. Student bodies still declare state-wide *bandhs* and strikes at the drop of a hat. All this gives currency to the idea that reading books is a pacifist activity and that real battles are to be fought on the street. It is a telling sign that today the North-East is cut off from India's high octane growth.

As teachers dispensing hope and wisdom, we must value the idea that education with a big dose of 'peace education' is the passport to the future.

At Maria's Public School we conduct classes on life-skills and I am happy to tell you that we have found children very receptive. We are also members of the *Gandhi Smriti Darshan Samiti* and in our own humble way we try to emphasize and spread the message that the answers to all conflicts need not be settled through aggression. The students have organized poster competitions, held debates and discussions and even run a marathon for peace. On Saturday 16th of February 2008 our little ones from class and 4 and 5 walked hand in hand with their grandparents from Janajatiya Field, Bonda to the school at Birkuchi with the message, "We Want Peace".

Dr. Savita Singh, Director of Gandhi Smriti commented very rightly that, "Peace is not merely the absence of conflicts but the ability to cope with it. Peace will continue to elude humanity till together they are able to craft a mechanism that can effectively prevent nations/people to resort to violence for political/personal goals".

I would like to end with a quote from the Father of the Nation – "I want to find peace in the midst of turmoil, light in the midst of darkness and hope in despair".

8

PEACE EDUCATION: IS IT NECESSARY?

*Mrs. Anjana Hazarika**

In every nook and corner when two people meet or in a get together or even when one talks to oneself, peace occupies the priority of discussions. Some people express a feeling of despair and sigh *Oh- the peaceful days are gone*! People often tend to shift the responsibility of peace to somebody else and talk about the degradation of moral values in the society. But the tragedy is that nobody realizes his own responsibility towards peace.

These are the common features in the society which I feel are worth mentioning here. People always try to exert influence on others by using their strength in terms of money, social status, physical strength etc. They are always judgmental in their behaviour towards their fellow beings.

We always see others. If we see a person with all material comfort we want it for ourselves. But how? To acquire it people follow both positive and negative paths. If anybody fails to have all these they remain dissatisfied. Dissatisfaction gives

*Principal, K.V., Khanapara, Guwahati-22

rise to jealousy – jealousy results in violence in thought and action.

This way, self interest is disturbed – dislike creeps in the mind and tendency to harm others arise. The joint family system has given way to the nuclear family system making people selfish and children are deprived of all good moral values that percolate down from the Grandparent to the child. The 'I' feeling i.e. ego regulates mind, giving no space for 'we'—*I must get everything. If I am not getting it, others also should not get. I am hit therefore I must hit back in retaliation. I am not successful – I will not allow others to succeed.*

Children do not understand the cruelties of life. They try to duplicate their seniors. As a result they also become a part of cruelty. The society is increasing in delinquent members who will soon shoulder the responsibility of the nation in future.

Who is responsible for the damage that poses serious threats not only to human society but to the whole world of living and non-living things?

This seminar has been arranged to discuss about the restoration of peace and whether peace education is the solution for it. If so, who should be trained and how? Should it be for new born and infants who are peaceful by birth or for the grown ups? Let us assume that it is necessary to train the young mind as they are the future of the society and nation at large. If it is so, it is pertinent to analyze the phases of life through which a child passes.

Indian epics illustrate the fact that an unborn child is emotionally and mentally alive and alert inside the mothers' womb. The present day psychologists also support this view. Thus it is necessary that expectant mothers should avoid violent ambiences – for personality grooming starts from here.

Three spheres make up man – the body, the mind and the soul. The outermost sphere of man is the body.

The second sphere is the mind which is the chariot of both negative and positive emotions.

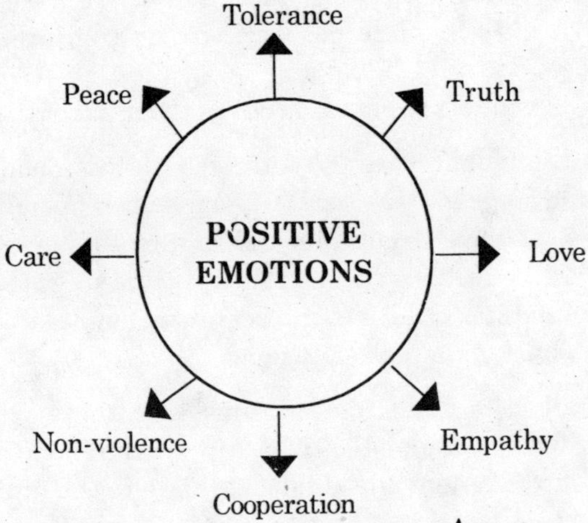

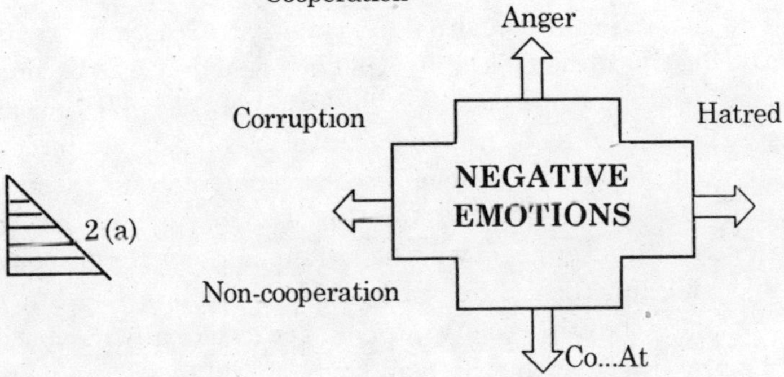

In the first phase he is confined to himself only. His actions are controlled and conditioned by his physical needs.

When he reaches the second phase he is able to relate to his family. His world revolves around his family members and interactions with them leave an everlasting impression in the mind of the child. At this stage, obeying rules, duplicating family members, inculcation of moral values carrying forward traditions and customs, mannerisms and habits are formed.

In the third phase the child is exposed to a bigger world. He is sent to school for formal education where he learns to adapt with his schoolmates, teachers and environment. Collective action and behaviour as desired by the school authority form another set of values in the mind of the child.

When the child is prepared to face life the door opens and the child steps into the society as a member. Social values here have some meaning for him and he starts understanding the concept of collective responsibility. By this stage the child begins to understand the meaning of mutual understanding, tolerance, sharing, and cooperation.

Gradually the child relates himself to the world and develops a feeling of global citizenship. At the highest level of mutual development the child can relate to the universe.

The period of transition from the 1st to 5th is very crucial. During this period if a child is not given guidance he becomes confused and conflicts arise. The mind of the child becomes perturbed and he begins to feel insecure. This gives birth to unhealthy thinking, unhealthy development and a diseased mind. Now it has become a matter of major concern that the minds of children teem with negative emotions. It may sound shocking but this is the reality. No matter how harsh it is, the fact is that the society has changed drastically. People do not practice what they preach. There is a rat race for material gain everywhere. It is paradoxical that with the increase in gadgets, life is becoming more insecure now. We have been robbed off peace. Parents rush to earn more to make the lives of their children comfortable but it is ironical that this comfort can lead to endless nights of suffering. The child remains perplexed. The young and impressionable minds are left with indifferent maids and sent to schools with an aim to mint money. This is the time when the child needs parental care. Difference in preaching and actions compels a child to be confused. The confused mind easily gets caught in peer pressure, often resulting in

- reluctance to go to school
- defiance
- indulgence in group fights
- drop outs
- restlessness
- insecurity

The most important question is who is responsible for it? It is none other than the parents and senior people of the society whom a child always tries to duplicate. There are instances where parents instigate the child to be revengeful reacting violently when they could not be more diplomatic in their own way. They themselves have a tendency to defy the rules and indulge in corruption. The ill effects on the young mind is aggravated by the media which often focus on negative news like corruption, ethnic clashes, political clashes, killings, kidnapping, torture of women etc. in the newspaper with photographs as well as repeat telecasts accompanied with sensational commentary.

All these negative news laced with sensational comments leave indelible marks on young and tender minds. Crimes by children are rising at an alarming rate. Campus violence is escalating. Tolerance level is narrowing down and heading towards invisibility. The general feeling observed daily among students is as follows:

Sl.	*Name*	*Complaint*	*Feeling*	*Punishments No.*
1	Sushan	Abused me	I felt very sad	I want him to suffer
2	Kishen	Cheated me	I felt miserable	Feel like punishing in some way
3	Shiva	Slapped me	I felt depressed	I want slap him very hard too
4	Karan	Bullied me	I was angry	I want Karan to get it from somebody

Simply discussing about these issues within the confines of the four walls cannot bring the solution to the problem. We always feel that something should be done, but who will do it? We try to find out the answer from others. Many a times, solutions to such problems involve trying out new ways within the educational institution thereby increasing the load of learning for the poor little mind of the child. Of course value oriented education should be there in the curriculum as the child is deprived of it, in the veritable rat race for the acquisition of material things by their parents. But there should be an attitudinal change in the mind of the people to reprogram oneself if peace is desired and to rescue the whole mankind from the clutches of war in any form external or internal.

We all live free lives-public, private & secret. In our public lives, we are seen and heard by colleagues, associates and others within our circle of influence. In our private lives, we interact more intimately with spouses, family members and close friends. Our real motives and desires are often kept secret from the public gaze. More often than not, we tend to live a hypocritical life. If we can remove the mask from our face I think the journey will be more comfortable.

Who is Rich & Who is Poor

One day

The father of a very wealthy family took his son on a trip to the country with the express purpose of showing him how poor people live. They spent a couple of days and nights on the farm of what would be considered a very poor family.

On their return from their trip, the father asked his son

How was the trip?

It was great, Dad.

Did you see how poor people live? The father asked.

Oh yeah, said the son.
So, tell me, what you learned from the trip? Asked the father.
The son answered:
I saw that we have one dog and they had four. We have a pool that reaches to the middle of our garden and they have a creek that has no end .....
We have imported lanterns in our garden and they have the stars at night.
Our patio reaches to the front yard and they have the whole horizon.
We have a small piece of land to live on and they have fields that go beyond .....
We have servants who serve us, but they serve others.
We buy our food, but they grow theirs.
We have walls around our property to protect us; they have friends to protect them.
The boy's father was speechless
Then his son added,
Thanks Dad for showing me how poor we are
Isn't perspective a wonderful thing?

We may never be strong enough to be entirely non-violent in thought, word and deed. But we must keep non-violence as our goal and make strong progress towards it.

"Most of us can read the writing on the wall; we just assume it's addressed to someone else." To conclude I must say ***"peace can not be taught it should be demonstrated".***

9

EDUCATION FOR PEACE

*Sawpon Dowreah**

The National Curriculum Framework (NCF) 2005 has identified a few National Concerns that require to be addressed by the school curriculum. Among them, Peace Education or education for peace has generated a great deal of interest because of its immediate relevance in the society of our time. We all know how important peace is for children's physical, moral, intellectual, spiritual and aesthetic development. What we perhaps need to know is how we can nurture peace where it is missing. The concept of Education for peace evolves from the Charter of the United Nations that was signed on the 26th June 1945 in San Francisco to prevent any global conflict in future. It reaffirms faith in the fundamental human rights leading us "to practice tolerance and live together in peace with one another as good neighbours." It also leads towards a culture of non-violence and tolerance in all walks of life to help in creating a peaceful and sane society.

The concepts of non-violence were the central theme of Gandhiji's total perspective of life. His entire life and actions

*Academic Officer, Board of Secondary Education, Assam

were an experiment on education for peace. He firmly believed that more than anything else, if we are to teach real peace in the world, we have to begin with children. In Gandhiji's belief, one can see an advocacy for education for peace. This concept raises a number of issues regarding the implementation of peace in schools. We have to address issues like –

- What is meant by peace?
- Why is it necessary for the school curriculum to address the concept?
- How can the secondary school curriculum address the concept?

As a starting point, it would be useful to consider what is meant by peace. Peace is often equated with absence of tensions, conflicts and all forms of violence including terrorism and war. Peace implies the capacity to live together in harmony. This calls for non-violent ways of resolving conflicts. Diversities can germinate into conflicts but conflicts need not necessarily germinate into violence. Peace is also equated with the creation of non-violent social systems. This implies the development of a society that is free from violence. Peace implies being aware of the meaning and significance of the word co-operation and also an awareness of how anger and violence can destroy peace. Further, peace is equated with absence of exploitation and injustice of every kind, ecological balance and conservation, and with adoption of life styles conducive to the spiritual and psychological peace.

These different perspectives of peace should help us in understanding the necessity for the school curriculum to address the issue of peace. It has been observed that peace implies a capacity to live together in harmony. Our education system should be able to develop in the learners, this important capacity. We cannot possibly think of a better way to develop this capacity than to integrate the concept in the curriculum if we seriously want our children to be equipped with the values, skills and attitudes they need to be able to live in harmony with others and as responsible citizens.

We live in a society that is marked by unprecedented violence, locally, nationally and globally. The violence that broke out in Beltola area in Guwahati barely two months ago is quite fresh in the consciousness of every one of us. Barely a week ago, NDTV (New Delhi Television) had broadcasted the unfortunate plight of a 15 year old schoolgirl from Delhi who was severely beaten by her class teacher for her decision to opt for a different private tutor and has been consequently lying in a hospital bed for more than a month in a state of coma. It is a serious matter considering that schools which are meant to be nurseries of peace, are becoming transmission points of violence.

It is not surprising therefore, that during the past few months the erstwhile Honourable Minister of Education, Assam, Sri Ripun Bora should receive a spate of letters from school children requesting him to consider including Rights of the Child in the curriculum. These letters are illustrative of a growing awareness among school children to the fact that like their adult counterparts, they also have the rights to love and affection, time and space to play, to be rescued first if a disaster takes place, free education, to grow up believing in peace and treating all people as brothers and sisters, special care for the disabled, proper housing, food and medical care, have name and nationality, become useful members of the society and enjoy all these rights without discrimination.

Indeed, education should aim at developing the values and skills in children to assert their rights which undoubtedly will lead them to a climate of peace and progress. Such awareness makes it clear that conflicts dissipate our collective energy and destroy the very structure of the quality of life. Every society in every age has acknowledged peace as a noble and necessary ideal and the school curriculum is the most appropriate forum for inculcating the notions of peace.

In the last few decades, the school curriculum had concerned itself with value education and moral education. One may wonder whether education for peace is a synonym for value education or moral education. However, it needs to be clarified that the concepts are not synonymous. Value education takes as its points of immediate concern a set of social, moral and ethical values. However, values become counter-productive when pursued in isolation from other values. What education for peace does is to look at social, moral and ethical values in a comprehensive framework. This leads us to the third and possibly the most crucial question: How can the concept of education for peace be addressed in the school curriculum?

It would be in order to begin with the Lower Primary level of education. At this level the focus is on inculcating the values and skills of education for peace with a view to laying the foundations for personality formation as well as developing the social skills necessary for living together in harmony. School activities have been geared to focus on –

- Cooperation i.e. working effectively with others towards a common goal.
- Adaptability i.e. willing to change opinions in the light of evidence and reason.
- Self-discipline i.e. ability to conduct oneself appropriately.
- Responsibility i.e. whatever be the nature of the task, students must be willing to assume a share of the responsibility.
- Respect for other people's views and opinions.

The class-work that pupils are required to do, the games that they play, the work-experience activities that they perform collectively are all centred in developing in pupils a spirit of co-operation, adaptability, self-discipline, responsibility and so on. These are key concepts in the curriculum for peace. It is possible to inculcate in pupils these values and attitudes through a series of group activities.

The next level of school education, the Upper Primary level builds on to the activities for the Lower Primary level by enabling pupils to see the culture of peace from the point of view of Indian History, philosophy and culture. A few years ago, there was a directive from the NCERT to the State and Central Boards of School Education to revise the history textbooks from the standpoint of national integration and necessary revisions were made to ensure that no sentiments of different communities were harmed through concepts in history textbooks. The whole approach was to look at the past in a more positive way.

Language textbooks can provide a strong foundation for integration of the concepts of Education for peace into the contents of the lessons which are essentially meant for the development of communication skills. A striking example of how peace dimensions are woven into a textbook lesson is "Rama's story" – a lesson included in the new English textbook for class VIII. The focus of the story is not merely on teaching communication skills but also on the process through which peace is achieved. The teacher can demonstrate to the class some of the ways by which one can show respect to others, demonstrate how pride and anger destroys peace and also demonstrate the changes that we need to bring about if we are to enjoy peace.

The Secondary School level focuses more on making the pupils aware of the need to make lifestyles conducive to the stability of the society. The students can be enabled to see the culture of peace from the standpoint of Human Rights, Fundamental Rights and Duties. These concepts in the Social Science textbook for class X should not be understood merely as instruction about human rights but as concepts encompassing a host of core and related values which promote a culture of peace, tolerance and sustainable development. These are the raw materials out of which social cohesion is produced and the soil in which peace strikes its roots.

Finally, it is important to state that the role of the teacher in the transaction of the concepts of peace in the classroom is a very crucial one. It follows from this that the teachers would require to orientate themselves not only in providing information about various aspects of human conflicts but also in teaching them the skills of developing a culture of peace. It remains the responsibility of the teacher to transform the thinking process of the students from violent solutions of various issues to non-violent processes. It is indeed a challenging task, but a task that can help in bringing ultimate peace on earth.

10

PEACE EDUCATION AND ITS NEED IN NORTHEAST INDIA: A Perceptive Investigation from Karbi Anglong and North Cachar Hills District of Assam

**Elizabeth Devi Kh.*

Conflict dates from the beginning of human history and will probably never end. Conflict is inherent in human growth and human development cannot proceed without conflict.[1] It can be a stimulus for positive development and action. With training, understanding and insight, positive outcomes can be achieved from conflict.[2] Conflict is a broad term and carries different connotations depending upon circumstances and behavioural responses of the parties involved. Conflict represents the persistent and pervasive nature of inter-group competition in which each party wishes to occupy a position that is incompatible with the wishes of the other and the parties are aware of the incompatibility of potential future positions. The experience of conflict is so basic that its negative

*Research Associate, Peace Studies, OKDISCD

effects spread to many aspects of community life. However, long term conflicts are likely to have long-term costs for the affected countries. The most destructive type of conflict such as inter-state, civil war and ethnic conflicts consists of violent mode of confrontation among adversaries.

"Poor societies are at risk of falling into no-exit cycles of conflict in which ineffective governance, societal conflict, humanitarian crisis and the lack of development perpetually chase one another" (Gurr, Marshall and Khosla).[3] Northeast India with its perennial socio-political turmoil in the garb of insurgency movements and inter-ethnic conflicts has been a bane in India's democracy. In Assam, one of the most prosperous and resource rich states of Northeast India, the incongruities between the ethnic Assamese aspirations to make Assam an 'independent state' and the poly-ethnic composition of the population has long been a persistent source of inter-ethnic conflicts.

It is a truism as mentioned by Collier that "the effects of violent conflict are likely to be experienced long after the fighting has stopped. Societies which have experienced violent conflict are in a sense geared up for war, and are more vulnerable to future violence than pre-conflict societies with similar risk factors".[4] This statement of Collier can very well be applied to the violence affected region of Northeast India in particular. According to Robben and Nordstorm, "at some level to be able to discuss violence, one must go to where violence occurs [and] research it as it take place".[5] This approach will enable for better understanding of what happened and generate findings which will be an immense help in policy prescription. Also, the knowledge of ground realities at hand will contribute in the understanding of the problem in a holistic manner. Besides, in analyzing these conflicts and to prevent mass violence, the social and economic conditions, cultural characteristics, psychological processes of groups and individuals that lead to it must be identified. It is pertinent to mention here that conflict is not the same as violence and the two should not be confused. In fact, the vast majority of human conflicts are resolved without violence.[6]

At a time when Peace Initiatives have left a big question mark, the need has been intently felt for peace-building to create awareness and train the common mass for solving problems in a peaceful manner without resorting to violence. Conceiving peace-building as the effort to strengthen the prospects of internal peace and decrease the likelihood of violent conflict, the overarching goal of peace-building is to enhance the indigenous capacity of a society to manage conflict without violence. It aims at building human security which is a concept that includes democratic governance, human rights, rule of law, sustainable development, equitable access to resources and environmental security.[7]

It is believed that durable peace and sustainable development can be achieved with peace education for developing the culture of peace by building right relationships and social structures through non-violence.

In objectivity, given the fact that armed conflicts have numerous causal factors and impacts and various stakeholders have a stake in their outcome, peace education cannot perform miracles. Peace education, alone is incapable of restoring a healthy peace to a society that has been damaged by violent conflicts but through peace education we can create awareness and train the common masses to facilitate the development of the common man to solve problems in a peaceful and democratic manner. Further, durable and sustainable peace can be addressed by peace education amongst groups and communities divided by hostility, deep rooted hatred, fear, anger, lost empathy, biased views *et al*. It has also been recognized as an important resource in the emergence of just and sustainable peace for bringing forward the "culture of peace" in trouble torn societies.

Essence of Peace Education: a cue from Karbi Anglong and North Cachar Hills district

Peace education as stated in Wikepedia Encyclopaedia is the process of acquiring the values, the knowledge and developing the attitudes, skills, and behaviors to live in harmony with oneself and with the other. The value of Peace education is emphasized in teaching nonviolence, love, compassion, trust, fairness, cooperation, respect, and a reverence for the human society and the environment. As communication is the pre-requisite for building bridges through mediation, contracts and all sorts of agreements, it is used as the core skill for imparting peace education. All in all, Peace education is an attempt to impart education according to the needs of the concerned society to deal with the enduring conflicts between groups by confronting ongoing injustice and resentment. It teaches people ways to not only understand and resolve conflicts but also ways to prevent conflict from escalating into subservient violence through values and knowledge that will pave towards establishing a "Peace culture" in the society.

With this perception the scholar as a member of the Peace Studies team of Omeo Kumar Das Institute of Social Change and Development, Guwahati, while coordinating a program titled "Pre-emptive Training in Peace Education- Theoretical and Activism Training" with special focus on Karbi Anglong and North Cachar Hills district of Assam (the two districts are mired in ongoing ethnic conflict and crisis of governance), came to the realization that Peace Education is a necessity. It was also realized that, for more reliability and inter-connection between the objectives of academic rigor and policy relevance, peace-building measures that actually engage with practice will be more relevant to the needs of practitioners and policy-makers.

Despite the diverse ways in which peace education is operationalised , in the contexts of intractable conflict as is experienced in these two districts it often entails elements of antiracism, conflict resolution, multiculturalism, cross-cultural training, and the cultivation of a generally peaceful outlook. It faces the most difficult obstacles, such as collectively held animosities, shared painful memories, and common national or ethnic views of self and of the other, all issues on a collective macro level. In fact these studies as compared with those pertaining to the micro level are least studied and conceptually less developed in the field of peace scholarship.[8]

Experiences and knowledge gathered from the field

In Karbi Anglong and North Cachar Hills district of Assam, violence has left an ugly mark in an otherwise peaceful society. Inspite of talks on peace and peaceful co-existence among the different communities residing in the two districts, we still see persistence of animosity among some of the ethnic communities like the Dimasa, Hmar, Karbi and Kuki communities. Besides, attacks by Karbi based militants on the Hindi speaking community often occur. The history of conflict in Karbi Anglong and North Cachar Hills district literally began after passing of the Assam Language Act and the demand for an autonomous state. But outright violence started with the formation of insurgent outfits like the Dima Halim Daogah (DHD) and United Peoples Democratic Solidarity (UPDS). Besides, objective and subjective interests over land, resources and social identity led to ethnic conflicts between Dimasa and Hmar ethnic groups in North Cachar Hills district in 2003. In the same pattern we have witnessed ethnic clashes between Karbi and Kuki communities in 2003 and between Karbis and Dimasas in 2005.

Under these circumstances, a peace training programme was conducted with different groups of society like women's groups and organisations, civil society groups, youth organisations, school going children, college students etc at different sub-divisions and blocks of Karbi Anglong and North

Cachar Hills district. While establishing relationships with different sections of the people in these two districts, it was felt that the people are basically peace-loving. The children especially took active part in all the programmes. They were excited to learn things that were not imparted in their schools. Through exchange of ideas and opinions, the children clearly stated that they were against any kind of violence. In the different camps that were held, they expressed their feelings in both the written form as well as through art.

The educational rationale and professional justification for conducting such camps for imparting peace education has a basis, relating to first, the nature of childhood socialisation to help them understand the world in which they live, and the interdependence of individuals, groups, and nations; second, the need for interactive education in a democratic society to help children to develop lively, enquiring minds, the ability to question and argue rationally; and third, value educational ideologies to instill respect for religious and moral values, and tolerance of other communities, traditions, and ways of life.

The experience the scholar had in a children's camp organized at Jirsong Asong, Diphu in Karbi Anglong on February 18th and 19th, 2008 with school students and their teachers from different sub-divisions and blocks of Karbi Anglong and N.C. Hills districts exemplifies how imparting peace education transforms an individual's outlook and behaviour towards one another.

"On the very first day, to be more exact within the very few hours, the feeling of discomfort could be sensed with the children belonging to the different/conflicting communities like Karbi, Kuki, Hmar and Dimasa. When it was enquired about the prevailing discomfort, they gave answers toned with diplomacy like....They were strangers, even the youngest in the camp was very diplomatic as he said pointing at a Karbi/Dimasa boy "He is not my friend"!

However, as the day matured the children were divided into several groups and they began interacting with one another while participating in different activities of the programme. This began to pay dividends. By the end of the day it was noticed that the initial discomfort between the children was fading. The next morning there were more surprises as it was found that overnight the children came to know so much about one another. It was confirmed that they were no more "strangers", as claimed by some children on the first day. This camp reveals the fact that if the impressionable minds of the younger generation is properly guided it would go a long way in evading future conflicts.

This camp revealed that the children seemed to have fairly well-defined ideas about conflict in the physical sense that is about outright violence—killings, beatings, burning of houses while it appears that they often had very hazy ideas about the nature of peace, especially regarding positive peace.

It is important to mention here that the children who participated in the camp made a point not to miss out on any of the cultural programmes. As participants they were trying to give in their best performance. They did not find any distinction on the basis of community or region. It maybe an oft repeated statement but cultural activities are one such approach that has the potential to cut across divisions and bind people together. In a culturally rich region like Northeast India involving people in cultural activities like music, theatre will bring people closer for more interaction which in the long run may help in minimizing differences among diverse groups.

Peace education in terms of Education for peace has to be child-centered (valuing the person) and reconstructionist (valuing positive peace), both of which seem particularly appropriate to the turmoil of the late twentieth century. Studying peace and conflict can therefore be justified by reference to the broad by agreed aims of education, to work on childhood socialisation, to the need for effective political education in a democratic society and to recognize longstanding traditions in education. It offers both a radical critique of much current educational practice but also clear indicators of how to change that practice. [9]

While conducting women's camps it was realized that organising such camps made the village women aware of their rights and issues starting from the family to the societal level. The women participants belonging to different communities and groups expressed their innermost feelings and shared their experiences with one another. Through such interactions, they could find a sense of belonging with one another and realized that as one group, they could achieve a lot. Peace education *inter alia* with group activities can be a platform for providing sustainable peace through interaction, communication and awareness in many aspects of the society. This is just one example and a single venture of expanding peace education informally involving people from the grass-roots level. This affirmation confirms that ventures on peace education in the wider aspect will help in bringing awareness, respect and understanding especially among conflicting groups/parties.

As research on peace and peace education has identified various approaches and its horizon broadened in today's world order, peace education *per se* should examine, with methods and contexts, which is more viable, compatible and closer to an individual's development, in particular and the society's commitment for non-violent mechanisms for solving problems, in general. For instance, Peace education as conflict mediation and transformation focuses on the analysis of conflict, from the personal to the global, and on ways of resolving such conflicts non-violently.[10] Much can be achieved with this approach with a checks and balance system by not reproducing inequality where an unequal balance of power exists.

Walford has prescribed that the aims of education for peace are to develop the knowledge, attitudes, and skills which are needed in order:

1) to explore concepts of peace both as a state of being and as an active process;
2) to enquire into the obstacles of peace and the causes of peacelessness, both in individuals, institutions, and societies;
3) to resolve conflicts in ways that will lead toward a less violent and a more just world;
4) to explore a range of different alternative futures, in particular ways of building a more just and sustainable world society.[11]

In the underlying context of peace education, more such efforts and exploration are needed in Northeast India to develop a focused way for imparting peace education in the regional context. The voyage of Peace Studies, Omeo Kumar Das Institute of Social Change and Development, Guwahati in undertaking a program for understanding and spreading Peace education as a trial venture in a span of one year is too short a period for a comprehensive development of the subject in the academic and policy relevance level. Therefore, more such initiatives have to be taken up for spreading the culture of peace in this conflict ridden region of Northeast India.

ENDNOTES

1. *International Encyclopaedia of the Social and Behavioural Sciences*, No.4, UK, 2001, p.2535
2. Santa Barbara, Jack & Santa Barbara, Joana, "Conflict Analysis", in MacQueen, Graeme (ed), (2004), *Making Peace:*

A Peace Education Manual for Afghanistan, Centre for Peace Studies, McMaster University, Canada, p.7.

3. Quoted in Goodhand, Jonathan (2006). *"Aiding Peace? The Role of NGOs in Armed Conflict",* Lynne Rienner Publishers, Colorado, p.28.

4. Quoted in *ibid,* p.28.

5. Quoted in *ibid,* p.5.

6. Santa Barbara, Jack and Santa Barbara, Joana, "Conflict Analysis", in MacQueen Graeme (ed), (2004), *Making Peace: A Peace Education Manual for Afghanistan,* Centre for Peace Studies, McMaster University, Canada, p.8.

7. Government of Canada, 2000, cited in Ball, 2002 quoted in Goodhand Jonathan (2006), *Aiding Peace? The Role of NGOs in Armed Conflict,* Lynne Rienner Publishers, Colorado, p. 12.

8. Salomon, Gavriel "*The Nature of Peace Education: Not all Programs are Created Equal*" in Saloman Gavriel & Nevo, Baruch (ed), (2002), *Peace Education—The Concept, Principles, and Practices Around the World",* Lawrence Erlbaum Associates, London.

9. Which way to Peace?, Peace Pledge Union, London.

10 *Ibid.*

11. *Ibid.*

PART–II

11

PEACE

The term **Peace** has multiple meanings and is multi-dimensional. The most common perception of *peace as an absence of war is known as **Negative Peace***. The notion of Negative Peace focuses on the absence of direct violence. The notion of a stable social order is a form of negative peace (Wenden, 1995 in Ho-Won Jeong, 2000: 24). Peace and conflict researcher Johan Galtung, proposed an alternate notion of peace, namely Positive Peace. ***Positive Peace** refers to social conditions involving the removal of not only direct violence but also structural violence*. According to Galtung, *Positive peace cannot be obtained without the development*

of just and equitable conditions associated with the elimination of non-egalitarian social structures (Galtung, 1969 in Ho-Won Jeong, 2000:25). For positive peace to be truly present in the society there should be equality, elimination of various forms of discrimination, freedom, autonomy, respect for nature, personal growth, economic equity etc.

12

CONFLICT

Conflict is inevitable. It has existed since time immemorial and will perhaps never end. According to a theorist, conflict can be described as 'a struggle over values and claims to scarce status, power and resources' (Boulding, 1962 in Ho-Won Jeong, 2008:5). Conflict arises from incompatibilities of interests and values. It is interwoven intimately with the social interactions amongst individuals in the society and thereby, its nature is multilayered and multi-dimensional. The nature of conflict can be Intra-personal, Inter-personal, Intra-group and Inter-group. At an individual level, not only do conflicts exist within the individual, they also exist outside the individual, governing the individual's social interactions. At a group level, conflicts can, not only exist within the members of the group, but can also exist between groups. The roots of the conflict may be manifold including among others, factors such as value differences, power disparities, socio-economic conditions, paucity of land /forest resources, immigration, threat to cultural identity etc.

13

CONFLICT RESOLUTION

Conflict resolution is the interdisciplinary study and learning of resolving conflict. Conflict can be managed and resolved through mutual agreements. In peaceful settlement, a common emphasis is placed on refraining from the threat or use of force. Academics and professionals concerned with the resolution of conflict draw from diverse fields of research. Conflict resolution as both a professional practice and academic field is highly sensitive to culture and is culture-specific. Successful conflict resolution usually involves fostering communication among disputants, problem solving, and drafting agreements that meet their underlying needs. Communication styles of the parties in conflict are culture specific. There are various strategies of Conflict Resolution such as Negotiation, Arbitration, Bargaining, Mediation, Conciliation, Problem-Solving process, Second-track diplomacy, Reconciliation among others.

- **Negotiation** is a process of one-to-one discussion that takes place among the conflicting parties with the goal of reaching an agreement.
- **Mediation** is a voluntary and confidential process in which a neutral third-party acts as a facilitator and helps the conflicting parties discuss difficult issues and

negotiate an agreement. Here, the mediator does not have the authority to issue any decision to settle the case. The conflicting parties in mediation create their own solutions.

- **Arbitration** is a process in which a neutral third-party, after reviewing evidence and listening to arguments from both sides, issues a decision to settle the case.
- **Mediation-Arbitration** is a hybrid that combines both of the above processes. Prior to the session, the disputing parties agree to try mediation first. But if mediation is not successful, arbitration is resorted to whereby the neutral third party gets the authority to make a decision.
- **Community Conferencing** is a structured conversation involving all members of a community (offenders, victims, family, friends, etc.) who have been affected by a dispute or a crime. Using a script, the facilitator invites people to express how they were affected and how they wish to address and repair the harm that resulted.
- **Negotiated Rulemaking** is a collaborative process in which government agencies seek input from a variety of stakeholders before issuing a new rule.
- **Peer Mediation** refers to a process in which young people act as mediators to help resolve disputes among their peers. The student mediators are trained and supervised by a teacher or another adult.

14

PEACEMAKING & PEACEKEEPING

PEACEMAKING

Peacemaking is a form of conflict resolution which focuses on establishing equal power relationships that will be strong enough to withstand the recurrence of future conflict, and establishing some means of agreeing on ethical decisions within a community that has previously had conflict. Mohandas Karamchand Gandhi is widely recognized as an important theorist of the peacemaking strategy. The term peacemaking however is reserved for large, systemic, often factional conflicts in which no member of the community can avoid involvement, and in which no faction or segment can claim to be completely innocent of the problems.

PEACEKEEPING

Peacekeeping is defined by United Nations as "a way to help countries torn by conflict create conditions for sustainable peace." Peacekeepers monitor and observe peace processes in post-conflict areas and assist ex-combatants in implementing the peace agreements they may have signed. Such assistance comes in many forms, including confidence-building measures, power-sharing arrangements, electoral support, strengthening the rule of law, and economic and social development. The Charter of United Nations gives the United Nations Security Council the power and responsibility to take collective action to maintain international peace and security.

15

NON-VIOLENCE

Non-violence as a concept has had a long and ancient tradition. The principle of non-violence was practised by many saints and philosophers of ancient times including Lord Buddha, Jesus Christ, Jain *Tithankaras*, Zoa Tsu and others. However, it was Mahatma Gandhi who for the first time in human history put forward the principle of non-violence to the common people so that they can practise it in their lives to resist evil and work for the welfare of the society.

The philosophy of non-violence speaks about how one must have love, sympathy and compassion for all, even for one's opponent. It is in this context that Gandhi made a distinction between the evil doer and his evil action so as to hate the sin and not the sinner. Non-violence advocates that one should not cause harm or injury either in word or deed to any living being, whether humans, animals or plants. It is important to note that true non-violence is a quality of the brave and not of the weak.

In order that common people can practise the principle of non-violence, Mahatma Gandhi devised the instrument of *Satyagraha*-which literally means "holding on to truth" (*satya* - truth and *grah*- hold on to something). *Satyagraha* involves two things - resisting evil and misrule through non-violent protests on the one hand and taking up constructive activities like handloom and handicraft, spreading the message of peace and brotherhood, on the other.

Non-violence was successful in helping India win independence from foreign rule. It also influenced and inspired the American Civil Rights Movement as well as the South African struggle against discrimination spearheaded by Dr. Nelson Mandela.

Gandhi leading a Satyagraha

16

PEACE EDUCATION

Peace Education is the process of acquiring the knowledge and developing the attitudes, and behaviour to live in harmony with oneself and with others. As a philosophy, its values incorporate the following:

- *Respect for others.*
- *Empathy*—Empathy is often characterized as the ability to "put oneself into another's shoes". It is defined as one's ability to recognize, perceive and experience what the other is experiencing.
- *Appreciation of and respect for diversity.*
- *Self-esteem*— Self-esteem is defined as a subjective evaluation of oneself, in a positive or negative manner. It finds expression in the form of beliefs, emotions and also behaviour.
- *Commitment to social justice* (it refers to the philosophy whereby individuals and groups within a society are accorded fair treatment and a just share of benefits), *equity* (fairness and impartiality) and *non-violence* (it refers to the philosophy that discourages the use of aggression and hostility to counter violent behaviour,

like wars and conflict. Instead it promotes peaceful means of resolving conflicts).

- *Concern for the environment and understanding of our place in the eco-system*—Efforts must be made to protect the natural environment. Unrestricted felling of trees and destruction of wildlife, have endangered large tracts of forest cover as well as our rich mineral and forest reserves. Thus, it is of utmost importance to understand the significance of keeping the symbiotic relation alive amongst all living forms in this planet.
- *Commitment to equality*—Equality can take different forms. Within a community, social equality refers to a state of affairs where different people are accorded the same status in a certain aspect, such as equal voting rights, freedom of speech, equal access to education, healthy facilities and basic infrastructure within the community etc.

Agenda for Peace Education

The Peace Education programme includes the need

1) To promote growth toward a community in which children are capable and desirous of open communication
2) To help children gain insights into the nature of human feelings and share their own feelings
3) To explore with children the unique personal ways in which they can respond to problems and begin to prevent or solve conflicts.

It is important to keep in mind that Peace Education takes different shapes as peace educators attempt to address forms of violence in different social contexts. The following five different types of Peace Education have been widely accepted by many.

1. **Human Rights Education**— Human Rights education can simply be understood as education based for honouring the basic dignity of all people. It includes multicultural understanding aimed at reducing stereotypes and hostilities between groups. Therefore, multicultural education is an essential element of education for peace to reduce the gap of cross-cultural ignorance which breeds enmity and hostility.

2. **Environmental Education**— The increasing effects of Global Warming, depleting natural esources and the extinction of several species of flora and fauna have made peace educators realize that it is not sufficient just to talk about violent conflicts, military security and protection of citizen's lives etc. They now recognize that it is equally important to promote the culture of peace based upon ecological security, where human beings are protected and nourished by natural processes.

3. **International Education**— This approach of Peace Education gives more importance to understanding international interstate systems that very often lead to wars and conflicts over territory , resources etc. It provides an understanding of how nation states construct security

for their citizens. It helps students to understand the positive and negative aspects of globalization, which has led to the erosion of power of national governments.

4. **Conflict Resolution Education**— The increasing level of violence that is happening in our society has motivated peace educators to develop and encourage conflict resolution education to help individuals understand conflict dynamics and empower them to use communication skills to build and manage peace relationships. Conflict resolution educators teach children human relations skills such as anger management, impulse control, emotional awareness, empathy development, assertiveness, and problem solving without using violence.

5. **Development Education:** Development studies is being included in Peace Education to help students gain insights into the various aspects of structural violence based on social institutions and traditions with propensities for dominance and oppression. For example, students in peace education classes learn about the plight of the poor and construct developmental strategies to address problems of structural violence.

17

HUMAN RIGHTS

Definition of Human Rights

- Human Rights are the fundamental natural rights which are the most precious possession of mankind and a world without them will have to face a perpetual risk of moral depredation.
- Broadly Human Rights can fall into i) Civil and Political rights

  ii) Economic, Social and Cultural rights
- These natural rights can not be taken away by any legislative measure anywhere.

Human rights refer to certain unchallengeable natural and universal rights of human beings regardless of factors such as nationality, religion, caste, creed, community and gender. Some of the Articles that are enshrined in the Universal Declaration of Human Rights that are important for us to live a life with dignity and integrity are as follows:

Article 1 All human beings are born free and equal in dignity and rights. They are endowed with reason and conscience and should act towards one another in a spirit of brotherhood.

Article 2 Everyone is entitled to all the rights and freedoms set forth in this Declaration, without distinction of any kind, such as race, colour, sex, language, religion, political or other opinion, national or social origin, property, birth or other status. Furthermore, no distinction shall be made on the basis of the political, jurisdictional or international status of the country or territory to which a person belongs, whether it is independent, trust, non-self-governing or under any other limitations of sovereignty.

Article 3 Everyone has the right to life, liberty and security of person.

Article 4 No one shall be held in slavery or servitude: slavery and the slave trade shall be prohibited in all their forms.

Article 5 No one shall be subjected to torture or to cruel, inhuman or degrading treatment or punishment.

Article 6 Everyone has the right to recognition everywhere as a person before the law.

Article 7 All are equal before the law and are entitled without any discrimination to equal protection of the law. All are entitled to equal protection against any discrimination in violation of this declaration and against any incitement to such discrimination.

Article 8 Everyone has the right to an effective remedy by the competent national tribunals for acts violating the fundamental rights granted to him by the constitution or by law.

Article 9 No one shall be subjected to arbitrary arrest, detention or exile.

Article 10 Everyone is entitled in full equality to a fair and public hearing by an independent and impartial tribunal, in the determination of his rights and obligations and of any criminal charge against him.

18

WOMEN'S RIGHTS

Millions of women throughout the world live in conditions of abject deprivation with attack against their fundamental human rights. The abuse and violence against women are relentless, systematic, and widely tolerated, if not explicitly condoned. The violence and discrimination against women are global and social epidemic, notwithstanding the very real progress of the international women's human rights movement in identifying and raising awareness about and challenging impunity for women's human rights violations. The women have the right to reject specific legal, cultural or religious practices by which they are systematically discriminated against and even excluded from political participation and public life. Groups like the Women's Rights Division of Human Rights Watch which is fighting against the dehumanization and marginalization of women, promotes women's equal rights and human dignity. Women's right is a global struggle based on universal human rights and the rule of law. Some of the constitutional guarantees for women in India are as follows.

The Constitution of India Guarantees to all Indian Women

Equality before the law, **Article 14**

No discrimination by the state on the grounds of religion, race, caste, sex, place of birth or any of these, **Article 15 (1)**

Special provision to be made by the state in favour of women and children, **Article 15 (3)**

Equality of opportunity for all citizens in matters relating to employment or appointment to any office under the state, **Article 16**

State policy to be directed to securing for men and women equally, the right to an adequate means of livelihood, **Article 39 (a)**

Equal pay for equal work for both men and women, **Article 39 (d)**

Provisions to be made by the state for securing just and humane conditions of work and for maternity relief, **Article 42**

To promote harmony and to renounce practices derogatory to the dignity of women, **Article 51 (A) (e)**

Freedom of thought and speech and the right to participate in decision making.

Milestones

Protection of Women from Domestic Violence Act 2005

Protection against Sexual Harassment of Women Act, 2005

Rape Evidence Act, The Criminal Procedure Code and The Indian Penal Code 73rd and 74th Constitutional Amendments, 1993

Women Engaging in Fishing to Earn their Livelihood

19

RIGHTS OF THE CHILD

Children like adults have the same general human rights. But they need certain special rights as they are particularly vulnerable. Despite the existence of rights, children suffer from poverty, homelessness, abuse, neglect, preventable diseases, unequal access to education and justice systems that do not recognize their special needs. Keeping in mind the special needs and rights of children, the Convention on the Rights of the Child sets out the rights that must be realized for children to develop their full potential by being free from hunger and want, neglect and abuse. The Convention offers a vision of the child as an individual and as a member of a family and community with rights and responsibilities appropriate to his or her age and stage of development.

In India, the post-independence era has experienced an unequivocal expression of the commitment of the government to the cause of children through constitutional provisions, policies, programs and legislation. The Constitution of India in Article 39 of the Directive Principles of State Policy pledges that "the State shall, in particular, direct its policy towards securing .... that the health and strength of workers, men and women, and the tender age of children are not abused, and that citizens are not forced by economic necessity to enter avocations unsuited to their age or strength, that children are given opportunities and facilities to develop in a healthy manner, and in conditions of freedom and dignity, and that childhood and youth are protected against exploitation, and against moral and material abandonment."

As a follow-up of this commitment and being a party to the UN declaration on the Rights of the Child 1959, India adopted the National Policy on Children in 1974. The policy reaffirmed the constitutional provisions and stated that "it shall be the policy of the State to provide adequate services to children, both before and after birth and through the period of growth to ensure their full physical, mental and social development. The State shall progressively increase the scope of such services so that within a reasonable time all children in the country enjoy optimum conditions for their balanced growth."

As the responsibility of children's nurture and proper growth is bestowed on the Government, children's programs have occupied a prominent place in the national plans for human resource development. Successive Five Year Plans have provided the wherewithal to deal with these issues. In the last decade of this century, dramatic technological developments particularly in the areas of health, nutrition, education and related spheres have opened up new vistas of opportunities for the cause of children.

India's Commitment towards Children's Rights

The Constitution of India, the National Policy for Children, many other policies and legislation accord priority to children's needs. The Government of India ratified the Convention on the Rights of the Child on 2nd December, 1992. Accordingly, the government is taking action to review the national and state legislation and bring it in line with the provisions of the Convention. It has also developed appropriate monitoring procedures to assess progress in implementing the Convention, involved all relevant government/ministries/departments, international agencies, non-governmental organizations, and the legal profession in the implementation and reporting process, publicized the Convention, and sought public inputs for frank and transparent reporting.

India is also a signatory to the World Declaration on the Survival, Protection and Development of Children. In pursuance of the commitment made at the World Summit, the Department of Women and Child Development under the Ministry of Human Resource Development has formulated a National Plan of Action for Children. Most of the recommendations of the World Summit Action Plan are reflected in India's National Plan of Action.

The National Plan of Action has been formulated keeping in mind the needs, rights and aspirations of 300 million children in the country and sets out quantifiable time limits for India's Charter of Action for Children by 2000 AD. The priority areas in the Plan are health, nutrition, education, water, sanitation and environment. The Plan gives special consideration to children in difficult circumstances and aims at providing a framework, for actualization of the objectives of the Convention in the Indian context. The National Plan of Action also lists out activities to achieve these goals. To make the aims and activities of the plan more need-based and area-specific, the Central Government has urged the State governments to prepare a Plan of Action for Children for their States, taking into account the regional disparities that may exist.

The Girl Child

The slogan of the Indian government for the Girl Child campaign was "A Happy Girl is the Future of our Country". Traditions, customs and social practices that place greater value on sons than on daughters, who are often viewed as an economic burden, still stand in the way of the girl child being able to achieve her full potential in India. A sustained educational campaign by the government and the NGOs has been started to ensure that baseless discrimination against the girl child is eliminated.

The Government of India has taken measures to protect and promote the Girl Child. It has announced its "Education for All" campaign which is to reach 19-24 million children in the age group 6-14, of whom 60 percent are girls. *A National Plan of Action for the Girl Child for 1991-2000* was also announced. This plan seeks to prevent female foeticide and infanticide, eliminate gender discrimination, provide safe drinking water and fodder near homes, rehabilitate and protect girls from exploitation, assault and abuse. The government's national policy of education and the Action Research Project on "The Girl Child and the Family" are also aimed at formulation of programs to improve the status of the girl child.

Street Children

It is estimated that there are 314,700 street children in Bombay, Calcutta, Madras, Kanpur, Bangalore and Hyderabad combined and about 100,000 in Delhi. Factors which have given rise to the increase in number of street children in India include poverty, family break-ups, armed conflicts, natural and man-made disasters, lack of employment opportunities and the attraction of cities.

Street Children have received much attention in the media, both national and international in the recent years. The awareness and sensitization efforts have led to several initiatives involving numerous groups working with street children, launching of specific schemes and programs at the local, state and national level and initiation of numerous studies on street children.

Non-Governmental Organizations or NGOs in India are doing laudable work in this area and are dealing with issues related to shelter, health, education and training of these children. A Central Scheme for the welfare of street children has recently been initiated by the Ministry of Welfare, Government of India. This scheme gives grant-in-aid to NGOs working on issues of street children.

India has also ratified the Convention on the Rights of the Child which came into force in 1990. This ratification implies that India will ensure wide awareness about Child issues among the government agencies, implementing agencies, the media, the judiciary, the public at large and the children themselves. The Government's endeavour is to create a conducive climate for acceptance of the goals of the Convention and to amend all legislation, policies and schemes to meet the standards set in the treaty framework.

Milestones:

The Child Labour (Prohibition and Regulation) Act, 1986

National Plan of Action on Children: The National Plan of Action represents India's response to the unprecedented opportunities which the present decade has ushered in, both through technological developments as well as a global ambience for redeeming India's age-old pledges. This Plan of Action identifies quantifiable targets in terms of major as well as supporting sectoral goals representing the needs and aspirations of 300 million children of India in the spheres of health, nutrition, education and related aspects of social support.

The goals of the National Plan of Action on Children include bringing about improvements in child health, in the health of expectant mothers, reduction in malnutrition, provision of and access to safe drinking water, universal enrolment of children in schools, ensuring a minimum level of learning, reduction of disparities and universalization of effective access to schooling, conservation and protection of the environment so that it is conducive to the health and well-being of children.

20

CO-EXISTENCE

Co-existence refers to the ability to live together with people belonging to different cultures and faiths. For example, in Assam, people belonging to different faiths like Christianity, Hinduism, Sikhism, Islam and Buddhism have co-existed peacefully for generations. Sometimes neighbouring countries which have an element of hostility between them are signatories to agreements that underlie the principle of Co-existence. The Five Principles of Peaceful Co-existence or Panchsheel are a series of agreements between People's Republic of China and India. In 1954, the two nations drew up Five Principles of Peaceful Existence:

1. Mutual respect for each other's territorial integrity and sovereignty.
2. Mutual non-aggression.
3. Mutual non-interference in each other's internal affairs.
4. Equality and mutual benefit.
5. Peaceful co-existence.

Inter-faith Dialogue

21

MULTICULTURALISM

Multiculturalism generally refers to a state of racial, cultural and ethnic diversity within the demographics of a specified place, usually at the scale of an organization such as school, business, neighbourhood, city or nation. Alternatively, it refers to the doctrine that several different cultures (rather than one national culture) can co-exist peacefully and equitably in a single country. India for example, is a multicultural entity and pluralism is a way of life for the people. People of various linguistic groups, religious faiths and cultural traditions intermingle and have peacefully co-existed for centuries. The same is true for the Northeastern region of India. It is home to several hundreds of ethnic groups with their own unique cultural traditions and way of life, creating a colourful mosaic of ethnic diversity. The notion of diversity is a positive force for a society's nationhood and cultural identity. Government multicultural policies may include:

- Recognition of multiple citizenship (the multiple citizenship itself usually results from the nationality laws of another country).
- Government support for newspapers, television and radio in minority languages.

- Support for minority festivals, holidays, and celebrations.
- Acceptance of traditional and religious dress in schools, the military, and society in general.
- Support for music and arts from minority cultures.
- Programs to encourage minority representation in politics, education, and the work force in general.
- Enforcement of different codes of law on members of each ethnic group (e.g. Malaysia enforces Sh'aria law, but only for a particular ethnic group)

22

TOLERANCE & COOPERATION

TOLERANCE

The term **Tolerance** refers to attitudes and practices that prohibit discrimination against those practices or group memberships that may be disapproved of by those in the majority. Conversely, **intolerance** may be used to refer to the discriminatory practices sought to be prohibited. Though developed to refer to the religious toleration of minority religious sects following the Protestant Reformation, these terms are increasingly used to refer to a wider range of tolerated practices and groups, such as the toleration of sexual practices and orientations, or of political parties or ideas widely considered objectionable.

COOPERATION

Cooperation is the process of working or acting together, which can be accomplished by both intentional and non-intentional agents. In its simplest form it involves things working in harmony, side by side, while in its more complicated forms, it can involve something as complex as the inner workings of a human being or even the social patterns of a nation. It is the alternative to working separately in competition. Cooperation may be *coerced* (forced), voluntary (freely chosen), or even unintentional, and consequently individuals and groups might cooperate even though they have almost nothing in common interests or goals. Examples of that can be found in market trade, military wars, families, workplaces, schools and prisons, and more generally any institution or organization of which individuals are a part (out of own choice, by law, or forced).

23

STEREOTYPE

A **Stereotype** is a simplified and/or standardized conception or image with specific meaning, often held in common by people about another group. A stereotype can be a conventional and oversimplified conception, opinion, or image, based on the assumption that there are attributes that members of the other group hold in common. Stereotypes are sometimes formed by a previous illusory correlation, a false association between two variables that are loosely if at all correlated. Stereotypes may be positive or negative in tone. Categorization and Association are two fundamental psychological concepts involved in stereotyping. In the process of Categorization, we tend to group people on the basis of easily identifiable characteristics such as age, race, and gender. This can happen outside of our awareness. In the process of Association, we tend to **stereotype** on the basis of sets of traits that usually go together or are associated with groups of people. Stereotypes can be based on language, skin colour, caste, class, race, gender, sexual identity, cultural identity etc. of a person. For example common stereotypes associated with India are that it is a land of snake-charmers, elephants and holy-men. **Negative stereotypes are called Prejudice**. Stereotypes are "standardized" and "simplified" conceptions of groups, based on some prior assumptions. They are created based on some idea of abstract familiarity. **Prejudices, on the other hand, are more specific - they are predispositions to differential behaviour patterns.**

Some of the *possible or likely* prejudicial effects of stereotypes are:

- Justification of ill-founded prejudices or ignorance
- Unwillingness to rethink one's attitudes and behaviour towards stereotyped groups
- Preventing some people of stereotyped groups from succeeding in activities or areas of interests.

24

GLOBALIZATION

In its literal sense, globalization is the process of transformation of local or regional things or phenomena into global ones. It can also be used to describe a process by which the people of the world are unified into a single society and function together. This process is a combination of economic, technological, socio-cultural and political forces (Croucher, 2004). Globalization is often used to refer to economic globalization, that is, integration of national economies into the international economy through trade, foreign direct investment, capital flows, migration, and the spread of technology (Bhagwati, 2004). Economic Globalization can be measured through the following parameters:

- Goods and services, e.g. exports plus imports as a proportion of national income or per capita of population
- Labour/people, e.g. net migration rates; inward or outward migration flows, weighted by population
- Capital, e.g. inward or outward direct investment as a proportion of national income or per head of population
- Technology, e.g. international research & development flows; proportion of populations (and rates of change

thereof) using particular inventions (especially 'factor-neutral' technological advances such as the telephone, motorcar, broadband)

Globalization is not limited only to the economic arena; it also incorporates the industrial, financial, political, ecological, informational, social, technology, transportation and cultural arena. Cultural exchanges and diffusion of the cultural identity are the hallmark of a globalized era.

25

SUSTAINABLE DEVELOPMENT

One of the important components of peace education is environment and sustainable development. In recent times, factors have contributed most directly to the excessive pressure on the environment and natural resources in the world: a doubling of the population over the decades; a tripling of the economic output; and the persistence of poverty. These pressures have been exacerbated by the recent economic downturn in the region, which has had economic and social consequences, inter alia on the capacity of some governments to implement planned activities relating to environmental protection and sustainable development.

Sustainable development is a pattern of resource use that aims to meet human needs while preserving the environment so that these needs can be met not only in the present, but in the indefinite future. The term sustainable development was used by the *Brundtland Commission* which coined what has become the most often-quoted definition of sustainable development as development that "meets the needs of the present without compromising the ability of future generations to meet their own needs". Sustainable development does not focus solely on environmental issues. Sustainable development can be conceptually broken into three parts: *environmental sustainability, economic sustainability* and *socio-political sustainability.*

Environmental sustainability is the process of making sure current processes of interaction with the environment are pursued with the idea of keeping the environment as pristine as naturally possible. Sustainability requires that human activity only uses nature's resources at a rate at which they can be replenished naturally.

Economic Sustainability identifies information, integration, and participation as key building blocks to help countries achieve development that recognizes these interdependent pillars. It emphasizes that in sustainable development everyone is a user and provider of information. It stresses the need to change from old sector-centered ways of doing business to new approaches that involve cross-sectoral co-ordination and the integration of environmental and social concerns into all development processes. Furthermore, it emphasizes that broad public participation in decision making is a fundamental prerequisite for achieving sustainable development.

26

GOVERNANCE

Governance

The process of decision making and implementation or non-implementation of the decisions refers to Governance. The Government is one of the participants in governance. Besides the Government, the other participators may include influential land lords, associations of peasant farmers, cooperatives, NGOs, research institutes, political parties, religious leaders etc. Good and effective governance can lead to development which in turn can lead to peace within the community.

For the Governance to be effective it should have several characteristics—

- Participation
- Rule of Law
- Transparency
- Accountability
- Protection of Human Rights
- Responsiveness

Governments which are characterized by these qualities are bound to have less corruption and greater transparency in its functioning. The term transparency means openness and accountability. It implies that information about the functioning of the Government is freely available and accessible to all who are affected by it.

27

THE RIGHT TO INFORMATION ACT (RTI)

The Government of India has enacted the Right to Information Act, 2005 which came into effect from October 12, 2005. The implementation of the Act gives the citizens of India access to information under the control of public authorities to promote transparency and accountability in these organizations. However, under Section 8 and 9 of the Act, certain categories of information are exempted from disclosure. This Act extends to the whole of India except the state of Jammu and Kashmir (This is because Jammu and Kashmir has its own Constitution and thereby, also has its own Right to Information Act).

Under this Act, information can be obtained in material in any form including records, documents, memos, e-mails, opinions, advices, press release, circulars, orders, logbooks, contracts, reports, papers, samples, models, data material held in any electronic form and information relating to any private body which can be assessed by a public authority under any other law for the time being in force but does not include "file notings". All file notings are excluded except those relating to social and development sectors projects.

Now, a citizen of the country has the right to-

1) Inspect works, documents, and records.
2) Take notes, extracts or certified copies of documents or records.
3) Take certified samples of material.
4) Obtain information in the form of printouts, diskettes, floppies, tapes, video cassettes or in any other electronic mode or through printouts.

28

A CULTURE OF PEACE

The United Nations Educational, Scientific and Cultural Organization (UNESCO) has proposed certain elements as integral to a culture that fosters peace. They are as follows:

- Respect life.
- Practice active non violence.
- Share resources.
- Defend freedom of expression and cultural diversity.
- Protect nature
- Contribute to community development, especially including women and fostering democracy and solidarity.
- Cultural transformation can be materialized through applied peace and reconciliation education to include:
    - Training in prejudice reduction, psychological healing and social skills development.
    - Promotion of democratic tradition and human rights.
    - Deglorification of victory, winning and violence.

- Promotion of dialogues, wider participation and public consultations.
- Promotion of pluralism (as opposed to dominance of one culture and assimilation into it).
- Promotion of basic human needs for all (as non-negotiable rights)
- Bringing out the fears and hopes of all parties through dialogues and consultations.
- Promotion of empathy and compassion towards others.
- Promotion of non-violence as a conflict resolution and problem solving approach to replace violent actions.

29

WORLD FAMOUS PEACEMAKERS

Mohandas Karamchand Gandhi

"You must be the change you want to see in the world."

-Mahatama Gandhi

Mohandas Karamchand Gandhi, commonly known in India and across the world as Mahatma Gandhi (from *Sanskrit, mahātmā: Great Soul*) was born on *October 2, 1869* at *Porbandar, Gujarat*. He was the pioneer of *Satyagraha* — the resistance of *tyranny* through mass *civil disobedience*, firmly founded upon *ahimsa* or total *non-violence* — which led India to independence from British rule and inspired movements for civil rights and freedom across the world. Gandhi turned non-violence into a tool which could be effectively used by the common people to resist tyranny and misrule.

As a British-educated lawyer, Gandhi first employed his ideas of peaceful civil disobedience in the Indian community's struggle for civil rights in South Africa. Upon his return to India, he organized poor farmers and labourers to protest against oppressive taxation and widespread discrimination. Assuming leadership of the *Indian National Congress*,

Gandhi led nationwide campaigns for the alleviation of poverty, for the liberation of women, for brotherhood amongst differing religions and ethnicities, for an end to *untouchability* and caste discrimination, and for the economic self-sufficiency of the nation, but above all for *Swaraj* — the independence of India from foreign domination. Gandhi famously led Indians in the disobedience of the salt tax on the 400 kilometre (248 miles) *Dandi Salt March* in 1930, and in an open call for the British to *Quit India* in 1942. He was imprisoned for many years on numerous occasions in botl. South Africa and India. Gandhi was assassinated on *January 30, 1948.*

Gandhi's life and teachings inspired *Dr. Martin Luther King Jr., Steve Biko* and *Aung San Suu Kyi* and through them the *American civil rights movement* and the freedom struggles in *South Africa* and *Myanmar* respectively.

MARTIN LUTHER KING JR.

Martin Luther King, Jr., (January 15, 1929-April 4, 1968) was born Michael Luther King, Jr., but later had his name changed to Martin. His grandfather began the family's long tenure as pastors of the Ebenezer Baptist Church in Atlanta, serving from 1914 to 1931; his father has served from then until the present, and from 1960 until his death Martin Luther acted as co-pastor. Martin Luther attended segregated public schools in Georgia, graduating from high school at the age of fifteen; he received the B. A. degree in 1948 from Morehouse College, a distinguished institution for African American of Atlanta from which both his father and grandfather had graduated. After three years of theological study at Crozer Theological Seminary in Pennsylvania where he was elected president of a predominantly white senior class, he was awarded the B.D. in 1951. With a fellowship won at Crozer, he enrolled in graduate studies at Boston University, completing his residence for the doctorate in 1953 and receiving the degree in 1955. In Boston he met and married Coretta Scott, a young woman of uncommon intellectual and artistic attainments.

In 1954, Martin Luther King accepted the pastoral of the Dexter Avenue Baptist Church in Montgomery, Alabama. Always a strong worker for civil rights for members of his race, King was, by this time, a member of the executive committee of the National Association for the Advancement of Colored People, the leading organization of its kind in the nation. He was ready, then, early in December, 1955, to accept the leadership of the first great African American nonviolent demonstration of contemporary times in the United States. The boycott organized by him lasted 382 days boycott was against the racial discrimination of the African Americans in the public buses of United Sates. On December 21, 1956, after the Supreme Court of the United States had declared the laws requiring segregation on buses was unconstitutional, the African Americans and whites rode the buses as equals. During these days of boycott, King was arrested, his home was bombed, he was subjected to personal abuse, but at the same time he emerged as a black leader of prominence.

In 1957 he was elected president of the Southern Christian Leadership Conference, an organization formed to provide new leadership for the now burgeoning civil rights movement. The ideals for this organization he took from Christianity; and its operational techniques from Gandhiji. In the eleven-year period between 1957 and 1968, King traveled over six million miles and spoke over twenty-five hundred times, appearing wherever there was injustice, protest, and action; and meanwhile he wrote five books as well as numerous articles. In these years, he led a massive protest in Birmingham, Alabama, that caught the attention of the entire world, providing what he called a coalition of conscience and inspiring his "Letter from a Birmingham Jail", a manifesto of the Black revolution; he planned the drives in Alabama for the registration of African Americans as voters; he directed the peaceful march on Washington, D.C., of 250,000 people to whom he delivered his address, "I Have a Dream", he conferred with President John F. Kennedy and campaigned for President Lyndon B. Johnson; he was arrested upwards of twenty times and assaulted at least four times; he was awarded five honorary degrees. He was named Man of the Year by *Time* magazine in 1963; and became not only the symbolic leader of American blacks but also a world figure.

In the year 1964, at the age of thirty-five, Martin Luther King, Jr., was the youngest man to have received the Nobel Peace Prize. When notified of his selection, he announced that he would turn over the prize money of $54,123 to the furtherance of the civil rights movement.

On the evening of April 4, 1968, while standing on the balcony of his motel room in Memphis, Tennessee, where he was to lead a protest march in sympathy with striking garbage workers of that city, he was assassinated.

AUNG SAN SUU KYI

The Nobel Peace Laureate 1991

In June 19, 1945 Aung San Suu Kyi was born in Rangoon. She was the third child in the family. Her name derived from "Aung San" from her father, "Kyi" from her mother and "Suu" from her grandmother.

Aung San, her father was the commander of the Burma Independence Army, and Ma Khin Kyi (later became Daw Khin Kyi) her mother, was a senior nurse of Rangoon General Hospital. In a July 19, 1947, General Aung San was assassinated. Suu Kyi was just two years old. Mother Daw Khin Kyi became a prominent public figure, heading social planning and social policy bodies in Burma. On January 4. 1948, the Independent Union of Burma was established. And in 1960 Daw Khin Kyi was appointed Burma's ambassador to India. Suu Kyi accompanied her mother to New Delhi, where, she did her higher studies in Lady Shri Ram College.

From 1964-67 Suu Kyi was in Oxford University, where she pursued her B.A. in philosophy, politics and economics at St. Hugh's College (elected Honorary Fellow, 1990). During this period she met her future husband Michael Aris.

In 1969 she went to New York for graduate study, staying with family friend Ma Than E, staff member at the United Nations, where U. Thant of Burma was the Secretary-General. Postponing studies, Suu Kyi joins U.N. secretariat as Assistant Secretary, Advisory Committee on Administrative and Budgetary Questions. During evenings and weekends, she volunteered at hospital, helping patients in programs of reading and companionship.

January 1, 1972 Suu Kyi married Michael Aris and joined him in the Himalayan kingdom of Bhutan, where he tutored the royal family and headed the Translation Department. There she became Research Officer in the Royal Ministry of Foreign Affairs.

In 1988 Suu Kyi moved to Burma to be besides her ailing mother. By August there was a mass uprising throughout the country against the dictatorship. Violent suppression by military killed thousands of Burmese. On August 15 Suu Kyi, in has first political action, sent an open letter to government, asking for formation of independent consultative committee to prepare multi-party elections. And on August 26 in her first public speech, Suu Kyi addressed several hundred thousand people outside Shwedagon Pagoda, calling for democratic government. Michael and her two sons were there with her.

By September 18 the military government established State Law and Order Restoration Council (SLORC). These led to, ban on Political gatherings of more than four persons. Arrests and sentencing without trial was reaffirmed. On September 24 National League for Democracy (NLD) was formed, with Suu Kyi as the general-secretary. The Policy of non-violence and civil disobedience was accepted by the party. During October-December, defying the ban, Suu Kyi made speech-making tours throughout the country to a large audience. On December 27 Suu Kyi's mother Daw Khin Kyi died at the age of seventy-six.

On January 2, 1989 the funeral of Daw Khin Kyi took place which was attended by a huge funeral procession. There Suu Kyi vowed that like her parents who served the people of Burma, so would she, even unto death. From January to July, Suu Kyi continued campaigning despite harassment, arrests and killings by the military regime. And on February 17 Suu Kyi was prohibited from standing for election. But this did not stop her from walking towards the rifled soldiers aiming at her in Irawaddy Delta in April of that year.

The military regime placed Suu Kyi under house arrest, without any charge or trial. Suu Kyi remained in detention, having rejected the offer to free her if she decided to leave

Burma and withdraw from politics. July 10, 1995 SLORC releases Suu Kyi from house arrest after six years of detention.

But her movements have still been restricted. While she has had some opportunities to telephone her family in England, she is regularly denounced in the government-controlled media, and there is concern for her personal safety. Efforts to revive any NLD party activities have been balked, and its members have been jailed and physically attacked. In the first months after detention was ended, she was able to speak to large gatherings of supporters outside her home, but this was stopped. Yet her popularity in the country has not diminished.

Internationally her voice has been heard not infrequently. Reporters with cameras and videotape have been able to interview her in person, and telephone interviews with the media outside Burma have also been published. Using video cassettes she has sent out statements, including the keynote address to the NGO Forum at the U.N. International Women's Conference in Beijing in August 1995.

There have been a number of visitors from abroad, including a member of the Norwegian Nobel Committee, whom she told that Norway will be the first country she will visit when free to travel. SLORC has changed its name to the State Peace and Development Council, but its repressive policies and violation of human rights continue unabated. Suu Kyi discourages tourists from visiting Burma and businessmen from investing in the country until it is free from the military regime. She finds hearing for such pleas among western nations, and the United States has applied economic sanctions against Burma, but Burma's neighbors follow their policy of not intervening in the internal affairs of other sovereign states, and Burma has been admitted into the Association of South Eastern Asian Nations.

On March 27, 1999, Michael Aris died of prostate cancer in London. He had petitioned the Burmese authorities to allow him to visit Suu Kyi one last time, but they had rejected his request. He had not seen her since a Christmas visit in 1995. The government always urged her to join her family abroad, but she knew that she would not be allowed to return to Burma again. This separation she regarded as one of the sacrifices she had had to make in order to work for a free Burma.

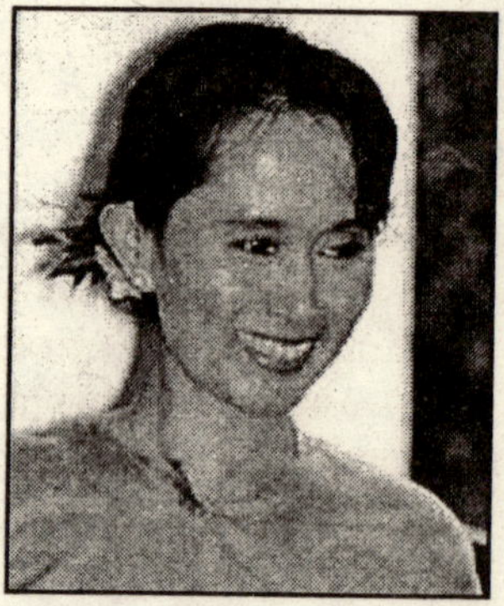

NELSON MANDELA

The Nobel Peace Laureate 1993

Nelson Rolihlahla Mandela was born in Transkei, South Africa on July 18, 1918. His father was Chief Henry Mandela of the Tembu Tribe. Mandela himself was educated at University College of Fort Hare and the University of Witwatersrand and qualified in law in 1942. He joined the African National Congress (ANC) in 1944 and was engaged in resistance against the ruling National Party's apartheid policies after 1948. He went on trial for treason during the period from 1956-1961 and was acquitted in 1961.

After the banning of the ANC in 1960, Nelson Mandela argued for the setting up of a military wing within the ANC. In June 1961, the ANC executive considered his proposal on the use of violent tactics and agreed that those members who wished to involve themselves in Mandela's campaign would not be stopped from doing so by the ANC. This led to the formation of Umkhonto we Sizwe. Mandela was arrested in 1962 and sentenced to five years' imprisonment with hard labour. In 1963, when many fellow leaders of the ANC and the Umkhonto we Sizwe were arrested, Mandela was brought to stand trial with them for plotting to overthrow the government by violence. His statement from the dock received considerable international publicity. On June 12, 1964, eight of the accused, including Mandela, were sentenced to life imprisonment. From 1964 to 1982, he was incarcerated at Robben Island Prison, off Cape Town; thereafter, he was at Pollsmoor Prison, nearby on the mainland.

During his years in prison, Nelson Mandela's reputation grew steadily. He was widely accepted as the most significant black leader in South Africa and became a potent symbol of resistance as the anti-apartheid movement gathered strength. He consistently refused to compromise his political position to obtain his freedom.

Nelson Mandela was released on February 11, 1990. After his release, he plunged himself wholeheartedly into his life's work, striving to attain the goals he and others had set out almost four decades earlier. In 1991, at the first national conference of the ANC held inside South Africa after the organization had been banned in 1960, Mandela was elected President of the ANC while his lifelong friend and colleague, Oliver Tambo, became the organization's National Chairperson.

WANGARI MAATHAI

The Nobel Peace Laureate 2004

Wangari Muta Maathai was born in Nyeri, Kenya (Africa) in 1940. She is the first African woman in East and Central Africa, to earn a doctorate degree. Wangari Maathai obtained a degree in Biological Sciences from Mount St. Scholastica College in Atchison, Kansas (1964). She subsequently earned a Master of Science degree from the University of Pittsburgh (1966). She pursued doctoral studies in Germany and the University of Nairobi, obtaining a Ph.D. (1971) from the University of Nairobi where she also taught veterinary anatomy. She became chair of the Department of Veterinary Anatomy and an associate professor in 1976 and 1977 respectively. In both cases, she was the first woman to attain those positions in the region. Wangari Maathai was active in the National Council of Women of Kenya in 1976-87 and was its chairman in 1981-87. It was while she served in the National Council of Women that she introduced the idea of planting trees with the people in 1976 and continued to develop it into a broad-based, grassroots organization whose main focus is the planting of trees with women groups in order to conserve the environment and improve their quality of life. However, through the Green Belt Movement she has assisted women in planting more than 20 million trees on their farms and on schools and church compounds. In 1986, the Movement established a Pan African Green Belt Network and has exposed over 40 individuals from other African countries to the approach.

Some of these individuals have established similar tree planting initiatives in their own countries or they use some of the Green Belt Movement methods to improve their efforts. So far some countries have successfully launched such initiatives in Africa (Tanzania, Uganda, Malawi, Lesotho, Ethiopia, Zimbabwe, etc). In September 1998, she launched a campaign of the Jubilee 2000 Coalition. She has embarked on new challenges, playing a leading global role as a co-chair of the Jubilee 2000 Africa Campaign, which seeks cancellation of the non-payable backlog debts of the poor countries in Africa by the year 2000. Her campaign against land grabbing and rapacious allocation of forests land has caught the limelight in the recent past.

Wangari Maathai is internationally recognized for her persistent struggle for democracy, human rights and environmental conservation. She has addressed the UN on several occasions and spoke on behalf of women at special sessions of the General Assembly for the five-year review of the earth summit. She served on the commission for Global Governance and Commission on the Future. She and the Green Belt Movement have received numerous awards, most notably The 2004 Nobel Peace Prize. Others include The Sophie Prize (2004), The Petra Kelly Prize for Environment (2004), The Conservation Scientist Award (2004), J. Sterling Morton Award (2004), WANGO Environment Award (2003), Outstanding Vision and Commitment Award (2002), Excellence Award from the Kenyan Community Abroad (2001), Golden Ark Award (1994), Juliet Hollister Award (2001), Jane Adams Leadership Award (1993), Edinburgh Medal (1993), The Hunger Project's Africa Prize for Leadership (1991), Goldman Environmental Prize (1991), the Woman of the World (1989), Windstar Award for the Environment (1988), Better World Society Award (1986), Right Livelihood Award (1984) and the Woman of the Year Award (1983). Professor Maathai was also listed on UNEP's Global 500 Hall of Fame and named one of the 100 heroines of the world. In June 1997, Wangari was elected by Earth Times as one of 100 persons in the world who have made a difference in the environmental arena. Professor Maathai has also received honorary doctoral degrees from several institutions around the world: William's College, MA, USA

(1990), Hobart & William Smith Colleges (1994), University of Norway (1997) and Yale University (2004). Professor Maathai serves on the boards of several organizations including the UN Secretary General's Advisory Board on Disarmament, The Jane Goodall Institute, Women and Environment Development Organization (WEDO), World Learning for International Development, Green Cross International, Environment Liaison Center International, the WorldWIDE Network of Women in Environmental Work and National Council of Women of Kenya. In December 2002, Professor Maathai was elected to parliament with an overwhelming 98% of the vote. She was subsequently appointed by the president, as Assistant Minister for Environment, Natural Resources and Wildlife in Kenya's ninth parliament.

MOHAMED ELBARADEI

The Nobel Peace Laureate 2005

Dr. Mohamed ElBaradei is the Director General of the International Atomic Energy Agency (IAEA), an intergovernmental organization that is part of the United Nations system. He was appointed to the office effective 1 December 1997, and reappointed to a third term in September 2005. From 1984, Dr. ElBaradei was a senior staff member of the IAEA Secretariat, holding a number of high-level policy positions, including the Agency's Legal Adviser and subsequently Assistant Director General for External Relations.

Dr. ElBaradei was born in Cairo, Egypt, in 1942, son of the late Mostafa ElBaradei, a lawyer and former President of the Egyptian Bar Association. He gained a Bachelor's degree in Law in 1962 at the University of Cairo and a Doctorate in International Law at the New York University School of Law in 1974. He began his career in the Egyptian Diplomatic Service in 1964, serving on two occasions in the Permanent Missions of Egypt to the United Nations in New York and Geneva, in charge of political, legal and arms control issues. From 1974 to 1978 he was a special assistant to the Foreign Minister of Egypt. In 1980 he left the Diplomatic Service to join the United Nations and became a senior fellow in charge of the International Law Program at the United Nations Institute for Training and Research. From 1981 to 1987 he was also an Adjunct Professor of International Law at the New York University School of Law.

During his career as diplomat, international civil servant and scholar, Dr. ElBaradei has become closely familiar with the work and processes of international organizations, particularly in the fields of international peace and security and international development. He has lectured widely in the fields of international law, international organizations, arms control and the peaceful uses of nuclear energy, and is the author of various articles and books on these subjects. He belongs to a number of professional associations, including the International Law Association and the American Society of International Law.

In October 2005, Dr. ElBaradei and the IAEA were jointly awarded the Nobel Peace Prize for efforts "to prevent nuclear energy from being used for military purposes and to ensure that nuclear energy for peaceful purposes is used in the safest possible way." In addition, he has received multiple other awards for his work. These include the International Four Freedoms award from the Roosevelt Institute, the James Park Morton Interfaith Award, and the Golden Plate Award from the Academy of Achievement. Dr. ElBaradei is also the recipient of a number of honorary degrees and decorations, including a Doctorate of Laws from New York University and the Nile Collar – the highest Egyptian decoration.

HIS HOLINESS THE DALAI LAMA

Tenzin Gyatso, born on July 6, 1935, is the fourteenth and current Dalai Lama. On November 17, 1950, at the young age of fifteen, he was crowned as Tibet's Head of State. During that period, Tibet was facing occupation by the forces of the People's Republic of China. After the collapse of the Tibetan Resistance Movement in 1959, Tenzin Gyatso (The Dalai Lama) fled to India, where he took up steps to establish the Central Tibetan Administration (which is the Tibetan Government in exile) in Dharamshala, in India. Today, Dharamshala has emerged as a centre for the preservation of Tibetan culture and education amongst the thousands of refugees that have settled there. The Dalai Lama has been successful in publicizing the demand for a Free Tibet, around the world. In recognition for the work he has done for his people and his non-violent struggle for the emancipation of people's rights, he was awarded the Nobel Peace Prize in 1989. His peace efforts continue till date.

MOTHER TERESA

Mother Teresa was born as Agnes Gonxa Bojaxhiu in Albania, on 26 August 1910. She dedicated her life to working with the poor and needy on the streets of Kolkata. She founded the Missionaries of Charity and for over forty years, tended to the needs of the poor, sick, orphaned and dying of Kolkata. By the 1970s, she became internationally famous as a humanitarian and an activist for the poor and the helpless. In 1979, Mother Teresa was awarded the Nobel Peace Prize for her humanitarian work. Following her death in 1997, she was officially recognized by Pope John Paul II as Blessed Teresa of Calcutta.

PART–III

30

PERSPECTIVES ON PEACE: LOOKING THROUGH THE LENS OF CHILDREN AND ADOLESCENTS

*Triveni Goswami**

'Mahatma Gandhi is Peace!' These were the words of a young child who was asked to define what peace was to him, in a school camp. The project *'Pre-emptive Training in Peace Education: Theoretical and Activism Training'* aimed at creating awareness on the notion of peace education at the grassroots. The project covered the autonomous district councils of Karbi Anglong and North Cachar Hills in Assam and the target group included children, youth, women and civil society organizations. As part of the project, workshops as well as school camps were organized with children and adolescents from these two districts. The underlying theme of these workshops was the notion of Peace and a special attempt was made to tap the young minds, to delineate their perspectives on peace and conflict. In total, seven (7) such

*Triveni Goswami is a Research Associate at Peace Studies, OKDISCD

camps were organized in different places (Manja, Harangajao, Mahur, Sarihajan, Lajorijan, Diphu) within the jurisdiction of the two districts of Karbi Anglong and North Cachar Hills. During these camps they were involved in various activities such as Singing Songs on themes related to peace, love and friendship; Essay Writing; Art work; Group Discussions; Games etc. The children and adolescents in these camps belonged to various ethnic communities and came from both rural as well as urban based schools.

The last camp in the series was a 2-day camp, organized in Diphu—the administrative headquarters of Karbi Anglong. In this camp, the participants comprised of both school students as well as their teachers from different sub-divisions and blocks of Karbi Anglong and North Cachar Hills district. The students ranged from Class II to Class XI and they belonged to diverse ethnic communities such as *Karbi, Dimasa, Hmar, Bengali, Nepali, Assamese, Kuki and Jaintia.* The responses of the children and adolescents were in the written form as well as reproductions in art.

A review of literature of the research carried out on children's perspectives on peace and conflict reveals that children internalize through their interactions with their environment and thus, the cultural environment they grow in, influence their understanding of the notions of peace and conflict. Children are in a continuous process of developing their ideas of what constitutes peace and conflict.

A study carried out by Robin Hall, covering 608 students aged 4-16 years in 10 government schools in New South Wales, Australia, confirmed several findings of previous studies while rejecting many others. The study sought to explore the following questions—*What factors influence children's cognitive and affective constructions of war and peace? And specifically, how do children's thoughts and feelings about these concepts vary with age, gender and selected aspects of the socialization process, especially type of school attended, sources of information about war and peace, and feelings of security?*[1]

Table reflecting the findings of the study carried out by Hall and other comparable studies on Children's Perspectives on War and Peace[2]

	Previous Studies	*Robin Hall's Study*
Age	• Knowledge of war/peace increases with age (Cooper)	• Confirmed
	• Children know more about war than peace (Cooper, Alvik)	• Not Confirmed • Confirmed
	• 'Meaningfulness' and images increase with age (Haaverlsrud)	• There is a J-shaped age curve of acceptance of war
	• Acceptance of war increases with age (Cooper)	• Confirmed
	• There is a U-shaped age curve of acceptance of war (Tolley)	• Confirmed
	• Very young children have attitudes about war but may not be able to verbalize them (Rodd)	• Not confirmed
	• Belief in innate aggression increases with age (Haaverlsrud)	• Not confirmed
	• No relationship between violent defense and age	
Gender	• Girls talk more about war and are more threatened by it (Wahlstrom)	• Non-conclusive
	• Boys think warfare is intrinsic in human nature (Wahlstrom)	• Confirmed
	• Girls find war less necessary (Cooper)	• Confirmed

(Contd...)

	Previous Studies	*Robin Hall's Study*
	• Preschool boys know more about war than girls (Rodd)	• Confirmed
	• Girls are more likely to defend the home; boys the wider environment (Rosell)	• Not confirmed
	• There are no significant differences between the genders (Tolley, Haaverlsrud)	• Not confirmed
	• Girls have a lower level of interest in warfare (McKelvey)	• Non-conclusive
School Type	• Acceptance of war highest among children at military schools followed by Catholic and Public, least among Quaker schoolchildren (Tolley)	• Acceptance of war greatest among Private Protestant school children and boys at single-sex schools
	• No differences between senior secondary and vocational college students (Wahlstrom)	
Security	• Feeling insecure and threatened by war increased support for Vietnam War	• Feeling threatened associated with non-acceptance of war
Information sources/ Exposure to media violence	• Older children make use of greater range of sources (Alvik)	• Confirmed
	• TV is the most important source but family is also important (Connell)	• Not confirmed for Kindergarten –4; confirmed for years 6—10
	• Mass media the main source	
	• Parents' role is secondary (Tolley)	• Not confirmed for Years K-4
	• Children are more influenced by parents than teachers (McKelvey)	• Not confirmed for Years K-4
	• Exposure to media violence causes aggressive attitudes (Brock-Utne)	• Confirmed • Not Confirmed

Another study was conducted on *Children and Adolescents' Conceptions of Peace, War, and Strategies to*

Attain Peace: A Dutch Case Study by Ilse Hakvoort and Louis Oppenheimer. The study sought to explore the age-related changes in the conceptions children and adolescents hold about peace, war, and strategies to attain peace.

> The conceptions were assessed by means of a semi-structured questionnaire Presented to 101 Dutch children between 8 and 16 years of age and divided Into five age groups (mean ages 8, 10, 12, 14, and 16 years). Each age group consisted of approximately equal numbers of boys and girls to ascertain any gender differences. Developmental levels for children's understanding of the reciprocal nature of interpersonal relationships (assessed by means of role or perspective-taking tasks) were presumed to relate to their conceptions of peace and strategies to attain peace, in particular. In addition to a development from concrete, materially related conceptions to abstract, norm-related conceptions, the findings suggest a more complex developmental course. While 8 to 12 year olds used concrete, materially related characteristics for peace, war and strategies to attain peace, 14 to 16 year olds mentioned abstract, norm-related characteristics only when strategies to attain peace from an everyday perspective were considered. As noted by Selman, most 12 year old children understood the mutual or reciprocal nature of interpersonal relationships. The latter understanding was primarily associated with the more abstract, norm-related level of reasoning involving ideas about human attitudes and universal rights.[3]

Further research on these issues has revealed that with a greater understanding of politics, conceptions of war and peace too become concrete (Dijkman, 1987) for children and adolescents. A significant finding that emerged from various studies (Cooper, 1965; Hakvoort, 1989) was that the comprehension and verbal articulation of the concept of war was found to precede the concept of peace by several years in the children's development.[4]

Children's conceptions of peace are derived from the experiences with their social, political, cultural and physical environment. The environment that they find themselves in, have a major role to play in shaping their attitudes and opinions about life. Children growing up in an area ravaged by ethnic clashes and mindless killings get entangled in the hostile social interactions, which in turn, influence their behaviour and attitudes towards the 'other' in their community. According to Hakvoort (1996)[5], the views held by children are good indices of the prevailing norms, values, and attitudes towards peace in their society.

Several significant as well as interesting themes emerged from the present study, providing a deeper insight into the cognitive development of the mind of a young child and adolescent, caught amidst turmoil and traumatized by early experiences of loss and pain. The themes that have emerged revolve around their definition and understanding of peace.

Themes emerging from the Children's and Adolescents' perspectives on Peace

I. **Negative Peace** – One of the first responses, most children and adolescents came up with, is '*absence of war*'. The definition of peace as an absence of war is generally known as Negative Peace. Alternatively, children also came up with the notion of Non-violence. Although Non-violence per se has a multitude of meanings, for the developing, young mind of a child, Non-violence refers to an absence of violence and tension, thus connoting peace. Some of the responses of the children to the definition of peace were—*Absence of war; No fighting; Not fight with anyone else; No tension around* and *Non-violence.*

II. **Peace comes from within** — Many children and adolescents were of the view that peace was possible only if there was peace within each individual—internal peace as a pre-requisite of external peace. Some of the responses that emerged were *Peace should first be within oneself, only then can it be found within the family and society; Peace is within ourselves; Peace begins with ourself, only then can we show it to others.*

III. **Unity**—Themes revolving around the notion of Unity emerged in the course of our interaction with the children and adolescents. Many of them felt that unity within the community could play a significant role in establishing peace and the essence of harmonious relations and group work was focused upon. Some of the responses that emerged were—*United we stand, divided we fall; Peace is unity; Peace means co-operation, working at the grassroots; If only there is unity, can there be peace; When there is unity, there is love and when there is love, there is peace; Harmony with others; Peace means working together, helping each other, showing kindness and sympathy towards the other.*

IV. **The relation between Peace and Love**—The children and adolescents often equated the notion of peace with love. For them, love is a pre-requisite of peace. Some of the responses that emerged were—*Love and Peace are the same; Peace means love; Peace means to love each other; Peace is the sign of love, through which we can show gratitude towards our elders and Peace is the environment of love.*

V. **Essentiality of Peace**—They were of the opinion that peace is a necessity and that life could acquire its fullest meaning, only through it. Some of the responses that emerged were—*Peace is needed for all of us and Peace is most essential to live happily and comfortably.*

VI. **Respect**—The value of respect emerged strongly in their responses. The notion of respect not only was confined to oneself, but also to others in the society and more significantly towards elders. Some of the responses were as follows—*Good relations with elders; Love our district, state and country; Respect others; Respect different tribes and cultures and Respect oneself and the society.*

VII. **Values**—In their young minds, the children and adolescents linked the notion of Peace with several moral values that they had acquired through their experience at home and in school. Some of the values that they associated with peace were—*Truthfulness; Forgiveness; Sharing with others; Success; Honesty; Understanding each other; Think of others and be good to them; Make sacrifices; To be humble; Patience and Contentment.*

VIII. **Protection of the Environment**—Many of them were of the view that the protection of the eco-system was necessary to bring about peace. For them, loving the environment was as important as working to protect the environment, in the efforts to establish peace. Some of their responses were—*Peace means loving the environment; Stop hurting the animals and Loving and protecting the environment.*

IX. **Relation with Joy and Happiness** — The children and adolescents were of the view that peace could bring about joy and happiness.

X. **Peace Heroes** — For most youngsters that we interacted with, Mahatma Gandhi and Mother Teresa were their peace heroes. As one child stated, *Mahatma Gandhi is peace.*

XI. **Education as a precursor of Peace**—Some children and adolescents were also of the view that education is necessary for peace. A child has described *different stages to acquire knowledge on peace, namely—the Family, the School and the Society.*

The emergent themes reflect an emphasis on the role of moral as well as social values in shaping the definition of peace. It seems that for the impressionable, young mind of a child, *values such as sympathy, forgiveness, respect, love, unity, truth, honesty etc. play a major role in characterizing the essence of peace.* Children and adolescents in both these districts have been witness to a series of violent, ethnic clashes in the last couple of years and this perhaps, could be one of the main reasons for recognizing and placing such a great emphasis on the *need to establish peace in their communities.* The most common definition of peace articulated by them was 'absence of war'. According to Alvik and Cooper (1968), Cooper (1965), and Rosell (1968), children mostly perceive the concept of peace as a concrete situation without war or conflicts[6]. This conception of Peace is known as *Negative Peace.* Another important issue touched upon by the children and adolescents is the *need to protect the environment, as a way of establishing peace.* Of late, the frequency of conflicts occurring due to competition over scarce natural resources and encroachment of forest area by human beings has increased substantially, in this region. This has perhaps led the children and adolescents to articulate the inherent need of the society to *address issues concerning the environment as a means of establishing peaceful relations within the community.* The author is of the opinion that the children and the adolescents have focused on the notion of *peace within the individual* perhaps because *they belong to the Oriental culture which places due emphasis on spirituality and the need to introspect and look within oneself to search for peace.* The process of socialization may have played a role in the internalization of moral and social values within the specific cultural context. *Mahatma Gandhi and Mother Teresa* emerged as *popular peace heroes* for the children. The fact that they are often epitomized for their contributions to peacemaking in India possibly played a role in their names being mentioned by the children.

The issue of *Education as a pre-requisite of peace* too, was beautifully brought out by them through their responses. The role of Education in moulding young minds cannot be underplayed. In this age of turbulent political and social upheavals, education has a major role in shaping the attitudes and behaviours of both children and adults. In this respect, an understanding of the basic tenets of *peace education* can go a long way in not only addressing the fractures within the community but also in working towards strengthening the bonds that hold the community together.

Thus, we see that the children's and adolescents' conceptions of peace reflect the circumstances prevailing in the society and can prove to be crucial in formulating an understanding of and creating a framework for, addressing the inherent gaps in the community.

ENDNOTES

1. Hall, Robin (May 1993), How Children Think and Feel about War and Peace: An Australian Study, *Journal of Peace Research*, Volume 30, No.2, p. 181. http://www.jstor.org/stable/425198
2. *Ibid* p.183.
3. Hakvoort, I & Oppenheimer,L (1993) "Children and Adolescents' Conceptions of Peace, War, and Strategies to Attain Peace: A Dutch Study", *Journal of Peace Research*, Vol. 30, No. 1, p.65.
4. *Ibid*, p.73.
5. Hakvoort, I & Hagglund, S. *Giving Voice to Children's Perspectives on Peace* in Christie, D.J., Wagner, R.V., & Winter, D.A. (Eds), (2001), *Peace, Conflict, and Violence: Peace Psychology for the 21st Century*, Englewood Cliffs, New Jersey: Prentice Hall.
6. Hakvoort, I & Oppenheimer,L (1993), "Children and Adolescents' Conceptions of Peace, War, and Strategies to Attain Peace: A Dutch Study", *Journal of Peace Research*, Vol.30, No. 1, p.66.

31

CHILDREN'S AND ADOLESCENTS' REPRODUCTIONS IN ART

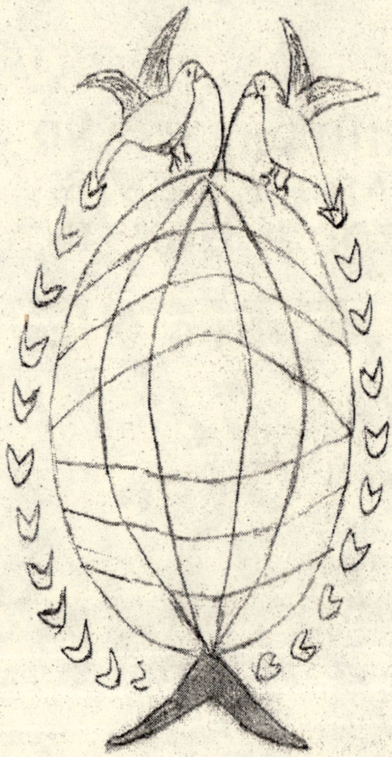

Art by,

Puja Sutradhar

From: Nightingale English High School, Manja

Title: Oline leaf symbol of peace

Art by,
Socila Phangchopi
Chokihala High School
Karbi Anglong District

HELPING FOR OTHERS

Art by,

Gobin Rongphar

School–Saint Xavier

PEACE & LOVE

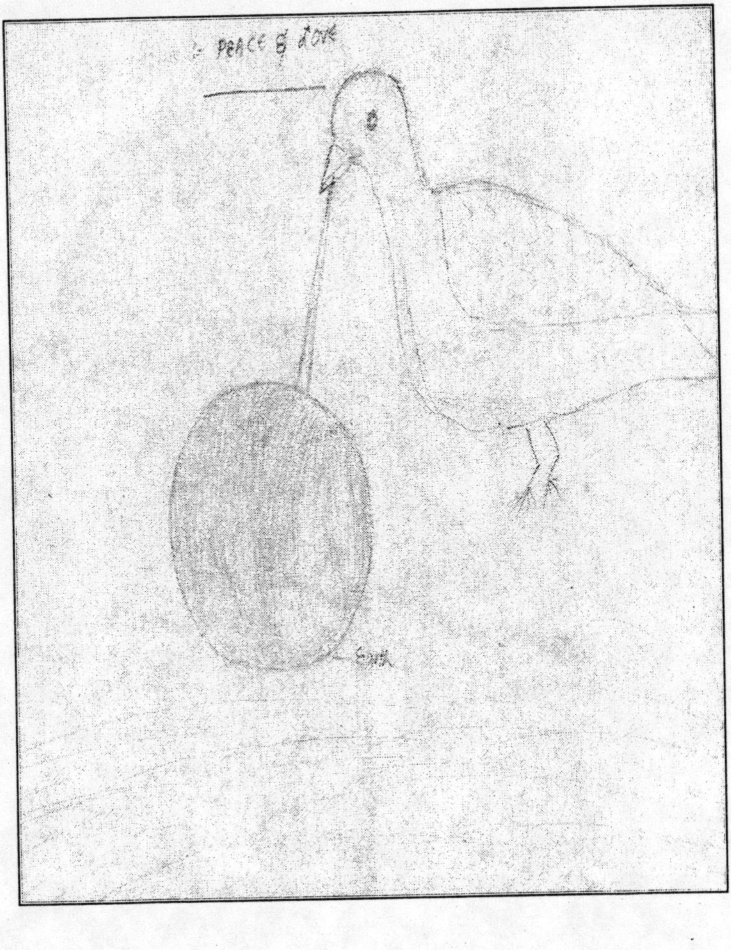

PEACE IS POSSIBLE

Art by,
Vindinor Hansepi
Assumption English School,
Chokihala, Karbi Anglong District

PART–IV

EXERCISES/ACTIVITIES

Exercise 1: "Listen carefully" (This is an important step in the process of dialogue in any conflict situation and attempts to resolve the same):

Ask four students to volunteer. Split them into two groups-Group A and Group B, with two students in each group. Ask one student form each group to tell the other student about a recent experience, which he found interesting. E.g. something he saw on TV, a wedding, a demonstration, a journey, etc. For Group A, tell the other student secretly not to pay attention to what is being told. Ask him or her to look in other directions, to lean backwards, and close his eyes and by the use of body language, to show that he is not interested in the story. In case of Group B, secretly tell the other student to listen very carefully to what is being told, to show great interest, to keep nodding, lean slightly forward and to show signs of really listening. Ask the class to carefully record the reactions and flow of communication in each case and solicit their views on the whole exercise.

Tell the students that active listening is an important pre-requisite of the dialogue process.

Exercise 2: Exploring Assumptions

Ask the students to pair up in twos. Then write four to five of the following questions on the blackboard:

- Numbers of family members?
- Place you were born?
- Favourite subject?
- Favourite hobby?
- Favourite music?
- Favourite colour?
- Favourite place?

Ask the students to guess the other person's likely answers to the questions and then get the correct answers. This is done to show how it feels to have to make assumptions about another person and to feel how it is to have assumptions made about oneself. The teacher should make these points clear to all the students at the end of the interviews. After the group work, ask the students to discuss in class:

How did it feel to have to make assumptions about your classmates?

How did it feel to have assumptions made about oneself?

Exercise 3: To identify the different ways to react to a conflict:

Explain to the students that there are many different ways to react to the conflicts listed on the blackboard and that everybody has their own way or style of reacting when confronted in a conflict. Some of the more common reactions to conflicts can be categorized as follows (write the words in bold on the blackboard)-

"My way or the Highway"

(*E.g. Refusing to have it any other way than our own*)

Aggression

(*E.g. Turning to violence to solve the conflict*)

Compromising

(*E.g. Both parties give something and both parties gain something*)

Accommodating

(*E.g. Letting the other person get his/her way*)

Avoiding, Delaying or Denying

(*E.g. Leaving the conflict issue and showing that it is of no importance*)

Appealing to others/getting help

(E.g. *Ask an uninvolved party to solve the conflict*)

While writing these on the blackboard tell the students that it is important to realize that none of these are "the best way to react"-any given situation calls for a unique solution and reaction. However, some of these reactions, especially aggression, can be argued to have very limited or no qualities as a means to solve conflicts.

Read the following stories to the class or hand them out to the students. Divide the students in groups and ask them to find out which of the reactions on the blackboard is most suited for a given conflict situation. Some of the conflict situations are mentioned below:

You meet one of your classmates on a busy street in Diphu town when you are walking with your friends-you are in a hurry to catch a movie. Right away he starts accusing you of cheating by copying his answers in the latest math test-a test where you for the first time scored high marks. You did not cheat but really studied hard, but he won't listen and starts screaming. How do you react?

(E.g.: Avoiding, delaying or Denying. The reason is that this is not the time or place to start arguing and you can bring it up later if you want to offer him an explanation)

You and your friends want to play some football one afternoon after school. You have gathered enough players to have two teams and you head off to the only football field in the neighbourhood. When you get there, you are arrive at the same time as a big group of boys also wanting to play. They claim that they have just as much right to be there as you do and they start arguing and look very threatening. How do you react?

(E.g. Compromising. The reason is that you both have the same right to be there-no one came before the other and no one wants to leave.)

You and another friend would like to watch a movie. You really want to see the latest English movie because everybody talks about it in class. Your friend does not understand English that well and he would prefer the newest Hindi movie instead. He states his point and you state yours. How do you react?

(E.g. Accommodating. The reason is that your friend's argument is sincere. You won't lose that much by accommodating)

Your mother wants you to take the garbage out right after dinner, but this is the same time as your favourite programme begins. Your show only lasts 30 minutes and taking garbage out takes about 10 minutes. Your mother wants you to do this because she wants the kitchen cleaned after dinner. How do you react?

(E.g.; Collaborating. The reason is that you also have to do your chores around the house. You could work out a plan where she could put the garbage by the door and you can take it out after your TV programme.)

Exercise 4: **Jumping off the violence escalator** (how to deescalate a conflict that has already started to escalate and is turning violent):

Ask the students the following questions and write their suggestions on the left side of the blackboard:

- How can you deescalate a violent conflict where you are the angry one?

Possible answers might be:

Try to cool down the way that works best for you.(E.g. Count to ten)

Share your feelings about the conflict with the other person.

Explain your point of view

Refuse to use violence

- How can you deescalate a violent conflict where the other person is the angry one?

Possible answers might be..

Ask about the other person's feelings about the situation and practice active

Listening.

Don't get defensive in any way.

Encourage the other person to keep talking as this gets the anger to dissipate.

Walk away and leave the scene.

Don't act violently.

Don't use abusive language.

Keep an open mind all the time.

Exercise 5: To learn that not all conflicts have to have a winner and loser-conflicts can end in win-win situations:

Ask two students to volunteer. It is important that the

students are more or less of the same bodily size and are of the same gender. Ask them to position themselves in an arm wrestling position-but point out this is not arm-wrestling but a similar game.

The idea of the game is that the one who gets the other person's hand to the table wins one point. They continue this for about 30 seconds. The winner is the one who gets 20 points-make a point of telling the students this. No talking between the two is allowed during the game.

After the 30 seconds, none of them has got points enough to win-there is no winner.

Then whisper to the two wrestlers, secretly without the rest of the class hearing it, that if they take turns in letting each other push their hands down, they would both win.

Ask them to play again in front of the class for another 30 seconds to show the rest of the class that both teams can win.

After the 30 seconds, both teams have got 10 points and both teams are winners.

Ask the students:

What happened in the two games?

What was the difference between the two games?

It is important that the following points are made:

The first was played as a struggle

The second was played with cooperation

The first game was played against each other

The second game was played together.

ANNEXURES

HANDOUT I 1-1

CONCEPTIONS OF PEACE

Directions: Read each quote and list elements necessay for a peaceful society:

Quotes	*Elements necessary for a peaceful society*

1. **You cannot simultaneously prevent and prepare for war.**
2. **War cannot be humanized it can only be abolished.**
   -*Albert Einstein* (1870-1955) physicist, anti-war activist, awarded the Nobel Prize in Physics in 1922
3. **All Humanity is one undivided and indivisible family, and each one of us is responsible for the misdeeds of all others.**
4. **There is no way to Peace Peace is the way.**
   -*Mahatma Gndhi* (1869-1948) Indian leader of satyagrah, theory and practice of nonviolent resistance. He led the peaceful Indian resistance to British rule.
5. **If you are Neutral in Situations of Injustice, you have Chosen the side of the oppressor.**
6. **If the World could end apartheid the world can end war.**
   -*Archbishop* (Ret.) *Desmond Tutu* (1931) Johannesburg, South Africa, founder of the Truth and Reconciliation Commission, awarded the Nobel Peace Prize in 1984.
7. **The Good we secure for ourselves is precarious and uncertain until it is secured for**

Quotes	*Elements necessary for a peaceful society*

all of us and incorporated into our common life.
-Jane Addans (1860-1935) founder of the social settlement Hill House n Chinago in 1919. She was awarded the Nobel Peace Prize in 1931.

8. **There is no trust more sacred than the one the world holds with children. There is no duty more important than ensuring that their rights are respected, that their welfare is protected. That their livers are free from fear and want and that they grow up on peace.**
Kofi A. Annan, (1938-) Secretary-General of the United Nations.

9. **Peace Begins when the Hungry are fed.**
-Anonymous

10. **In Separateness lies the World's Great Misery; in compassion lies the World's True Strength.**
-The Buddha. Founder of the Buddhist philosophy, born around 565 B.C. in Nepal. Buddha means "enlightened one".

11. **Wars Make Poor Tools for Carving out Peaceful Tomorrows.**
-Martin Luther King. Jr. (1929-1968) U.S. Christian Minister and leader of the U.S. civil rights movement, awarded the Nobel Peace Prize in 1964.

12. **It is not Power that Corrupts, but Fear. Fear of Losing Power Corrupts those who Wield it and Fear of the Scourge of Power**

Corrupts those who are Subject to it.

-Aung San Suu Kyi (1945-) Leader of the democracy movement in Burma, awarded the Nobel Peace Prize in 1991. She was the democratically elected President, and in a *coup d'etat* was arrested and remains under house arrest.

13. **It isn't Enough to Talk about Peace. One Must Believe in it and it isn't Enough to Believe in it. One Must Work at it.**

    -Eleanor Roosevelt (1884-1962), American human rights activist, stateswoman, journalist, educator, author, diplomat. First lady of the United States (1933-1945). She chaired the committee that drafted and approved the UN Universal Declarations of Human Rights.

14. **The Pacifist's Task Today is to find a Method of Helping and Healing which Provides a Revolutionary Constructive Substitute for War.**

    -Vera Brittain, (1893-1970) Pacifist, best known for her book *Testament of Youth,* in which she tells the story of her harrowing experience in the First World War.

15. **Peace in not the Product of a Victory or a Command. It has no Finishing Line, No Final Deadline, no Fixed Definition of Achievement. Peace is a Never-ending Process, the Work of Many Decisions.**

    -Oscar Arias (1941-) Born in the United States. President of Costa

Quotes	*Elements necessary for a peaceful society*
Rica from 1986-1990, mediated a peace agreement in Nicaragua and received the Nobel Peace Prize in 1987. Re-elected President in January, 2006.	
16. **For the Concept of a War-free World to Become Universally Accepted and Consclously Adopted by Making War Illegal, A Process of Education will be Required at all levels; Education for Peace, Education for World Citizenship. War is not an Inherent Element in Human Society.** -*Sir Jozef Rotblat* (1908-2005), Polish-born British physicist, Nobel Peace Prize 1995 for his efforts towards nuclear disarmament. One of the most prominent critics of the nuclear arms race, he signed the Russell-Einstein Manifesto in 1955 and was knighted in 1998.	

REFERENCE

Balantic, J & Libresco, A.S. (Eds), *Peace Lessons from Around the World* Produced in Cooperation with the International Advisory Committee of the Global Campaign for Peace Education. Hague Appeal for Peace, pp. 14-15 *www.haguepeace.org*

HANDOUT I 4-1

RESEARCH GUIDE–TELEVISION VIOLENCE

Directions Select a television program popular with young people. Watch three episodes of the show and record data in the chart below:

Name of Show____

Type of Show____

Day and Time of Show________________________________

Type of Violence	*Tally of Occurrences*	*Comments*
Yelling		
Swearing		
Threatening		
Bullying		
Hitting		
Kidnapping		
Using Weapons		
Physical Assault		
Killing		
Bombing		

- How would you characterize your results? Did they surprise you?
- How might young people be affected by viewing these programs on a regular basis?

REFERENCE

Balantic, J & Libresco, A.S. (Eds), *Peace Lessons from Around the World* Produced in Cooperation with the International Advisory Committee of the Global Campaign for Peace Education. Hague Appeal for Peace, pp. 28-29, *www.haguepeace.org*

HANDOUT IV 1-1

DEFINING SECURITY

Directions: Read each definition of security.[1] Create a symbol or illustration to represent each definition. Which aspects of security are most important to you, your community, our nation and the world?

Definitions of Security	*Illustration / Symbol*
Physical Security–nourishment, clothing and shelter that provide protection from the elments; protection from disease; treatment for illness; a certainty that an individual's basic needs will be met.	
Preventive Security–orderliness, rules, and consistent protection from physical harm, abuse, violence, and terror.	
Emotional Security–a sense of belonging and being loved and cared for; feelings of acceptance from others; healthy interpersonal relationships with family, friends, adults, peers, and co-workers.	
Development Security–access to education; the opportunity and freedom to learn, achieve, and contribute to society.	
Cultural Security–affirmation of cultural identity, values, and traditions; respect for and legal protection of a person's ethnic, recial, religious, and gender identity; freedom to participate as full partners in society regardless of cultural identity.	
Political Security–the degree of protection and safety that a government provides its citizen within a nation;	

1. Source: www.esrnational.org/sp/we/uw/security/htm

Definitions of Security	*Illustration / Symbol*
protection from threats beyond a nation's borders; the quality and degree of civil rights and civic participatin in decision-making.	
Economic Security–access to training and the development of useful skills; access to jobs and wages which provide a decent standard of living; provision of benefits for the aged, the sick, the disabled and children.	
Environment Security–protection from environmental hazards and toxins; provisions for safe and clean air, water, and food supplies; provision for a safe, clean habitat.	
National Security–development and maintenance of weaponry; military preparedness, recruiting and training of military personnel, military budget.	

HANDOUT IV 1-2

INVESTIGATING SECURITY IN OUR COMMUNITY, NATION AND WORLD

Directions Read each definition of security.Create a symbol or illustration to represent each definition. Which aspects of security are most important to you, your community, our natino and the world?

Aspect of Security

____

____

Evidence

- ____
- ____
- ____
- ____
- ____
- ____
- ____
- ____
- ____
- ____

REFERENCE

Balantic, J & Libresco, A.S. (Eds) *Peace Lessons from Around the World* Produced in Cooperation with the International Advisory Committee of the Global Campaign for Peace Education. Hague Appeal for Peace, pp. 99-100 *www.haguepeace.org*

HANDOUT II 3-1

WANGARI MAATHAI'S NOBEL PEACE PRIZE ACCEPTANCE SPEECH, 2004

As I was growing up [in rural Kenya], I witnessed forests being cleared and replaced by commercial plantations, which destroyed local biodiversity and the capacity of the forests to conserve water.

In 1977, when we started the Green Belt Movement, I was partly responding to needs identified by rural women, namely lack of firewood, clean drinking water, balanced diets, shelter and income.

Throughout Africa, women are the primary caretakers, holding significant responsibility for tilling the land and feeding their families. As a result, they are often the first to become aware of environmental damage as resources become scarce and incapable of sustaining their families.

The women we worked with recounted that unlike in the past, they were unable to meet their basic needs. This was due to the degradation of their immediate environments as well as the introduction of commercial farming, which replaced the growing of household food crops. But international trade controlled the price of the exports from these small-scale farmers and a reasonable and just income could not be guaranteed. I came to understand that when the environment is destroyed, plundered or mismanaged, we undermine our quality of life and that of future generations.

Tree planting became a natural choice to address some of the initial basic needs identified by women. Also, tree planting is simple, attainable, and guarantees quick, successful results within a reasonable amount of time. This sustains interest and commitment.

So, together, we have planted over thirty million trees that provide fuel, food, shelter, and income to support their children's education and household needs. The activity also creates employment and improves soils and watersheds. Through their involvement, women gain some degree of power over their lives, especially their social and economic position and relevance in the family. This work continues.

Initially, the work was difficult because historically our people have been persuaded to believe that because they are poor, they lack not only capital, but also knowledge and skills to address their challenges. Instead they are conditioned to believe that solution to their problems must come from 'outside'. Further, women did not realize that meeting their needs depended on their environment being healthy and well managed. They were also unaware that a degraded environment leads to a scramble for scarce resources and may culminate in poverty and even conflict. They were also unaware of the injustice of international economic arrangements.

...the tree became a symbol for the democratic struggle in Kenya. Citizens were mobilized to challenge widespread abuses of power, corruption and environment mismanagement. In Nairobi's Uhuru Park, at Freedom Corner, and in many parts of the country, trees of peace were planted to demand the release of prisoners of conscience and a peaceful transition to democracy. Through the Green Belt Movement, thousands of ordinary citizen were mobilized and empowered to take action and effect change. They learned to overcome fear and a sense of helplessness and moved to defend democratic rights.

In time, the tree also became a symbol for peace and conflict-resolution, especially during ethnic conflicts in Kenya when the Green Belt Movement used peace trees to reconcile disputing communities. During the ongoing re-writing of the Kenyan constitution, similar trees of peace were planted in many parts of the country to promote a culture of peace. Using trees as a symbol of peace is in keeping with a widespread African tradition. For example, the elders of the Kikuyu carried a staff from the thigi tree that, when placed between two disputing sides, caused them to stop fighting and seek reconciliation. Many communities in Africa have these traditions.

Such practices are part of an extensive cultural heritage, which contributes both to the conservation of habitats and to cultures of peace. The Green Belt Movement exports the concept of cultures biodiversity, especially with respect to indigenous seeds and medicinal plants.

As we progressively understood the causes of environment degradation, we saw the need for good governance. Indeed, the state of any country's environment is a reflection of the kind of governance in place, and without good governance there can be no peace. Many countries, which have poor governance systems, are also likely to have conflicts and poor laws protecting the environment.

Today we are faced with a challenge that calls for a shift in our thinking, so that humanity stops threatening its life-support system. We are called to assist the Earth to heal her wounds and in the process heal our own–indeed, to embrace the whole creation in all its diversity, beauty and wonder. This will happen if we see the need to revive our sense of belonging to a larger family of life, with which we have shared our evolutionary process.

As I conclude I reflect on my childhood experience when I would visit a stream next to our home to fetch water for my mother. I would drink water straight from the stream. Today, over fifty years later, the stream has dried up, women walk long distances for water, which is not always clean, and children will never know what they have lost. The challenge is to restore the home of the tadpoles and give back to our children a world of beauty and wonder.

REFERENCE

Balantic, J & Libresco, A.S. (Eds), *Peace Lessons from Around the World* Produced in Cooperation with the International Advisory Committee of the Global Campaign for Peace Education. Hague Appeal for Peace, pp. 51-52, *www.haguepeace.org*

HANDOUT II 2-1

SAROJINI NAIDU

Directions Select a television program popular with young people. Watch three episodes of the show and record data in the chart below:

Read the quote below and answer the questions that follow.

Sarojini Naidu (1879-1949) is considered a pioneer of the women's movement in pre-independent India. She was president of the Indian National Congress and later became the first woman governor in free India.

From a Letter Written to Gopal Krishna Gokhale, Indian Nationalist, on December, 24, 1914

"Oh we want a new breed of men before India can be cleànsed of her disease. We want deeper sincerity of motive, a greater courage in speech and earnestness in action. We want men who love this country and are full of yearning to serve and succor their brothers and not to further aid in their degradation by insincerity and self-seeking...how tired I am of death, of the reiterated resolutions that have become almost meaningless by lip repetition: uncorroborated by the heart's conviction and unsustained by practical action..."

Questions

1. Who was Sarojini Naidu?
2. What did she mean when she wrote, "we want a new breed of men before India can be cleaned of her disease?
3. What does she mean when she says, "how tired I am of death, of the reiterated resolution that have become almost meaningless by lip repetition"?
4. Do you think her concerns about the effectiveness of resolutions could be applicable to other nations?

5. Based on her letter, what do you think she feared regarding the conditions of women in India?

HANDOUT II 2-2

EXCERPTS FROM THE INDIAN CONSTITUTION

Articles for the Protection of Women	*In Your Own Words*

Article 14. Equality before law

The State shall not deny to any person equality before the law or the equal protection of the laws within the territory of India.

Article 15. Prohibition of discrimination on grounds of religion, race, caste, sex, or place of birth

1. The State shall not discriminate against any citizen on grounds only of religion, race, caste, sex, place of birth...

2. No citizen shall, on grounds only of religion, race, caste, sex place of birth or any of them, be subject to any disability, liability, restriction or condition with regard to (a) access to shops, public restaurants, hotels and places of public entertainment: or (b) the use of wells, tanks, bathing ghats, roads and places of public resort maintained wholly or party out of State funds or dedicated to the use of the general public.

3. Nothing in this article shall prevent the State from making any special provision for women and children.

4. Nothing in this article...shall prevent the State from making any special provision for the advancement of any socially

educationally backward classes of citizens or for the Scheduled Castes and the Scheduled Tribes.

Article 16. Equality of opportunity in matters of public employment

Steps have to be taken by the government to improve the lot of the weaker sections of society and to prevent the exploitation of women and flowing from this basic right against exploitation and to be empowered are laws like the Dowry Prohibition Act, Maternity Benefits Act, laws for sexual harassment, special exceptions in the law for rape and sexual assault, Medical Termination of Pregnancy Act for abortion, cruelty or domestic violence under criminal law.

Article 21. Protection of life and personal liberty

No person shall be deprived of his life or personal liberty except according to procedure established by law.

Article 23. Prohibition of traffic in human beings and forced labour

1. Trafficking of human beings and beggars and other similar forms of forced labour are prohibited and any contravention of this provision shall be an offence punishable in accordance with law.

2. Northing in this article shall prevent the State from imposing compulsory service for public purposes, and in imposing such service the State shall not make any discrimination on grounds only of religion, race, caste or class or any

of them. Protective bodies against exploitation include: Constitution of National Human Rights Commission, Minority Commission, National Commission for Women..

HANDOUT II 2-3

STATISTICS OF WOMEN IN INDIA*

Population

- Total population: 1.03 billion (2001)
- Population of women: 496 million
- Population of men: 534 million
- Population of women in the population: 47.8%
- Population of men in the population: 52.2%
- Women generally make up 51% of a nation's population

Health: (1998-99)

- Infant Mortality for all the India: 540 deaths per 1,00,000 live births
- Infant Mortality in Rural areas: 619 deaths per 1,00,000 live births
- Infant Mortality in Urban areas: 267 deaths per 1,00,000 live births
- Percentage of births with a skilled attendant present: 43% (1995-2001)
- Maternal Mortality Rates in India are 100 times those of developed countries and significantly higher than developing countries like Sri Lanka, Vietnam and Cuba

Education and Employment

- For every 100 literate men, there are 61 literate women
- For every 100 boys enrolled in primary school, there are 83 girls enrolled (1995-1999)
- For every 100 boys enrolled in secondary school, there are 66 girls enrolled (1995-1999)
- The percentage of women working has risen from 13% in 1987 to 25% in 2001

---

*From: www.indianngos.com/issue/women/statistics/

- The percentage of women in senior management in India is 3%
- 90% of working women feel that they would continue working if their employers provided onsite child care

Government Positions Women Hold

- Less than 8% of Parliamentary seats
- Less than 6% of Cabinet positions
- Less than 4% of seats in High Courts and the Supreme Court

Violence

- In India every 26 minutes, a women is molested
- In India every 34 minutes, a women is raped
- In India every 42 minutes, an incident of sexual harassment takes place
- In India every 43 minutes, a women is kidnapped
- In India every 93 minutes, a women is killed

Questions

1. Draw conclusions about the position of women in India based on the statistics.
2. Write 3 questions that this data raises in your mind about the position of women in India.
3. Based on this data and your previous analysis of the Indian Constitution, discuss the extent to which the promise of the Constitution has been realized.

REFERENCE

Balantic, J & Libresco, A.S. (Eds), *Peace Lessons from Around the World* Produced in Cooperation with the International Advisory Committee of the Global Campaign for Peace Education. Hague Appeal for Peace, pp. 44-47, *www.haguepeace.org*

HANDOUT III 3-1C

AUNG SAN SUU KYI

(Nonviolent Pro-democracy Activist in Burma/ Myanmar)

Aung San Suu Kyi *quotes*

"The Democracy Process Provides for Political and Social Change without Violence".

"The Struggle for Democracy and Human Rights in Burma is a Struggle for Life and Dignity. It is a Struggle that Encompasses our Political, Social And Economic Aspirations".

"Please use your Liberty to Promote ours".

"Sometimes, 24 hours can bring a total Revolutionary Change".

"We will Prevail because our Cause is right, because our cause is Just...History is on our side. Time is on our side."

"I think by now I have made it fairly clear that I am not very happy with the word "hope" I don't believe in people just hoping. We work for what we want. I always say that one has no right to hope without endeavor, so we work to try and bring about the situation that is necessary for the country, and we are confident that we will get to the negotiation table at one time or another. This is the way all such situations pan out-even with the most truculent dictator".

REFERENCE

Balantic, J & Libresco, A.S. (Eds), *Peace Lessons from Around the World* Produced in Cooperation with the International Advisory Committee of the Global Campaign for Peace Education. Hague Appeal for Peace, pp. 84, *www.haguepeace.org*

REFERENCES

WEBSITES:

- http://en.wikipedia.org/wiki/Conflict_resolution
- http://en.wikipedia.org/wiki/Peacemaking
- http://en.wikipedia.org/wiki/Peacekeeping
- http://en.wikipedia.org/wiki/Nonviolence
- http://www.mkgandhi.org/nonviolence/index.htm
- http://en.wikipedia.org/wiki/Peace_education
- http://www.peaceeducation.org/
- http://www.peaceeducation.org.uk/
- http://www.efpinternational.org/index2.html
- http://en.wikipedia.org/wiki/Human_rights
- http://en.wikipedia.org/wiki/Women's_rights
- http://en.wikipedia.org/wiki/Children's_rights
- http://en.wikipedia.org/wiki/Peaceful_coexistence
- http://en.wikipedia.org/wiki/Multiculturalism

- http://en.wikipedia.org/wiki/Tolerance
- http://en.wikipedia.org/wiki/Stereotype
- http://en.wikipedia.org/wiki/Prejudice
- http://en.wikipedia.org/wiki/Globalization
- http://en.wikipedia.org/wiki/Sustainable_development
- http://en.wikipedia.org/wiki/Cooperation
- http://www.unescap.org/huset/gg/governance.htm
- http://www.nssd.net/country/nepal/nep03.htm
- http://en.wikipedia.org/wiki/Good_governance
- http://www.persmin.nic.in/RTI/welcomeRTI.htm
- http://www3.unesco.org/iycp/uk/uk_sum_cp.htm
- http://unesdoc.unesco.org/images/0012/001263/126398e.pdf
- http://en.wikipedia.org/wiki/Mother_Teresa
- http://nobelprize.org/nobel_prizes/peace/laureates/1979/teresa-bio.html
- http://www.dalailama.com/
- http://en.wikipedia.org/wiki/Dalai_Lama
- http://en.wikipedia.org/wiki/Wangari_Maathai
- http://nobelprize.org/nobel_prizes/peace/laureates/2004/maathai-bio.html

- http://www.mkgandhi.org/
- http://en.wikipedia.org/wiki/Mahatma_Gandhi
- http://nobelprize.org/nobel_prizes/peace/laureates/1964/king-bio.html
- http://en.wikipedia.org/wiki/Martin_Luther_King,_Jr.
- http://en.wikipedia.org/wiki/Aung_San_Suu_Kyi
- http://nobelprize.org/nobel_prizes/peace/laureates/1991/kyi-bio.html
- http://en.wikipedia.org/wiki/Nelson_Mandela
- http://nobelprize.org/nobel_prizes/peace/laureates/1993/mandela-bio.html
- http://en.wikipedia.org/wiki/Mohamed_ElBaradei
- http://nobelprize.org/nobel_prizes/peace/laureates/2005/elbaradei-bio.html

BOOKS:

- Hakvoort, I & Hagglund, S. *Giving Voice to Children's Perspectives on Peace* in Christie, D.J., Wagner, R.V., & Winter, D.A. (Eds) (2001) Peace, Conflict, and Violence: Peace Psychology for the 21st Century, Englewood Cliffs, New Jersey: Prentice Hall
- Pandey, S (Ed.) (2004) *Peace Education—Self Instructional Package for Teacher Educators*, National Council of Educational Research and Training, India
- Salomon, G & Nevo, B (Eds) (2002) *Peace Education: The Concept, Principles and Practices Around the World,* Lawrence Erlbaum Associates, London

- Reardon, Betty A (1988) *Comprehensive Peace Education: Educating for Global Responsibility,* Teachers College, Columbia University.

REPORTS

- Balantic J & Libresco, A.S. (Eds) *Peace Lessons From Around the World* Produced in Cooperation with the International Advisory Committee of the Global Campaign for Peace Education. Hague Appeal for Peace *www.haguepeace.org*
- *Peace Education Curriculum: An Introduction,* Centre for Dialogue and Reconciliation
- MacQueen, Graeme (Ed) (2004) *Making Peace: A Peace Education Manual for Afghanistan,* Centre for Peace Studies, McMaster University, Canada in cooperation with TRANSCEND www.humanities.mcmaster.ca/~peace

JOURNALS

- Hall, Robin (May, 1993) *How Children Think and Feel about War and Peace: An Australian Study,* Journal of Peace Research, Volume 30, No.2, http://www.jstor.org/stable/425198
- Hakvoort, I & Oppenheimer,L (1993) *Children and Adolescents' Conceptions of Peace, War, and Strategies to Attain Peace: A Dutch Study,* Journal of Peace Research, Vol.30, No. 1

THE PEACE STUDIES TEAM

Dr. Anuradha Dutta is currently Professor, Peace Studies, OKDISCD, Guwahati. Prior to this, she was Professor, Department of Political Science, Gauhati University for 35 long years. As a proficient academician and a social activist working on women and conflict issues, she has to her credit, a number of authored and co-authored books, articles and research papers on different socio-political issues. She is the co-editor of two publications –*Genesis of Conflict and Peace: Understanding Northeast India –Views and Reviews* and *Women and Peace: Chapters from Northeast India—Drawing the Unparallels The Known and the Unknown*

Elizabeth Devi Kh, a PhD Scholar and a social science researcher is presently working as a Research Associate, Peace Studies, OKDISCD and is working in the areas of Socio-political and Women issues, Conflicts and Peace Studies in Northeast India. She has to her credit studies on ULFA Insurgents of Assam, Political instability in Manipur, Muslim Women of Manipur and Peace-making, Electoral politics in Manipur. Besides, she has coordinated a multi-dimensional action-research project titled "Pre-emptive Training in Peace education: Theoretical and Activism Training". She is presently undertaking a study on *Women, Armed Conflict and its Impact: A Prismatic Analysis (a comparative study of Bodo Territorial Autonomous District & Karbi Anglong district of Assam).*

Prateeti Barman, Research Associate at Peace Studies, OKDISCD has completed her Bachelors and Masters in Social Work from Nirmala Niketan College of Social Work, Mumbai. In 2005, she was a Junior Research Fellow at OKDISCD and the title of her project was *Local Self-Governance, Civil Society and Peace Prospect: A case study* *of Nalbari district of Assam*. She has also presented research papers in national seminars. She is presently undertaking a study on *Civil Society and its Response to Insurgency in Assam: Case study of Nalbari, Kakopothar and Guwahati.*

Triveni Goswami, a Research Associate, Peace Studies, OKDISCD with post-graduation in Psychology from the University of Delhi, India was awarded the prestigious *UNESCO/Suzanne Mubarak/Japan-Egypt Friendship Fellowship for the Empowerment of Women in Peace and Gender Studies (2006 Cycle)* at Bibliotheca Alexandrina, Alexandria, Egypt. In 2005, as a Junior Research Fellow at the OKDISCD, she worked on a study on *Role of Women as Peace Builders with special reference to Nagaland*, which has since been published. Her recent publication is a book entitled *Gender & Conflict Transformation: Nagaland and Egypt* based on the work that she carried out in Egypt. A Rotary Peace Fellow, she has recently completed a 3 months Certificate course in the Rotary Peace and Conflict Studies Centre at Chulalongkorn University, Bangkok (January 2008 session). Currently she is engaged in a project on *Women Rebels: Revolutionizing Patriarchal Norms or Mere Puppets within the Organizational Structure?*

Urmimala Sengupta, Research Associate, Peace Studies, completed her Masters in Political Science from Gauhati University (GU) in 2007. She has presented research papers in several national seminars. She is presently undertaking a study on *An Initiative for Peaceful Coexistence: A Look into the Policies and Capacity Building Aspect among the Displaced Populace in BTADC, Assam.*